The Machine Shed Roots

We opened the Iowa Machine Shed Restaurant in 1978 in rural Davenport, Iowa with just over 100 seats. Our location wasn't great and much of the equipment was old (but clean) and broke too often.

We were all pretty young and green. But we started with a powerful commitment; that commitment was a simple five word constitution- "Dedicated to the Iowa Farmer." That dedication meant that we worked to have a restaurant that wasn't just "farm" themed but would be something that farmers could be proud of. That meant using only the best pork and beef, real whipped cream on the pies, hearty soups, fresh baked goods made from scratch, and little things like genuine mashed potatoes and real butter. Although we still had a lot to learn, that dedication guided us through the early days. Even though money was tight, we were never tempted to take a cheaper route.

Thanks to you, folks like The Machine Shed from the start. The original Machine shed has been expanded and improved many times. And now, other Machine Sheds have sprung up in Des Moines, Iowa; Olathe, Kansas; Rockford Illinois; Pewaukee and Appleton, Wisconsin. Along the way we have been delighted to have received a bushel basketful of honors from farm groups like the Pork Producers and the Beef Industry Council. We're constantly trying to live up to those honors on the food we prepare and in the way we prepare and the way we bring it to you.

Mike Whalen

Thanks for your help

Compliments of

Heart of America™
Restaurants & Inns™
True midwestern hospitality
Visit all of Heart of America's properties throughout the midwest

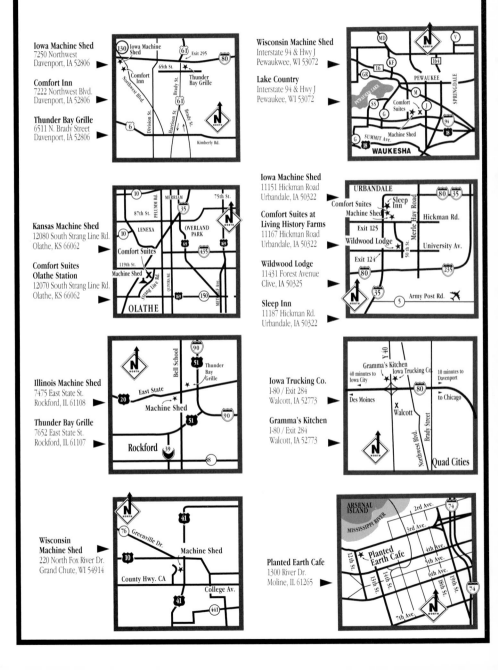

Iowa Machine Shed
7250 Northwest
Davenport, IA 52806

Comfort Inn
7222 Northwest Blvd.
Davenport, IA 52806

Thunder Bay Grille
6511 N. Brady Street
Davenport, IA 52806

Kansas Machine Shed
12080 South Strang Line Rd.
Olathe, KS 66062

Comfort Suites
Olathe Station
12070 South Strang Line Rd.
Olathe, KS 66062

Illinois Machine Shed
7475 East State St.
Rockford, IL 61108

Thunder Bay Grille
7652 East State St.
Rockford, IL 61107

Wisconsin Machine Shed
220 North Fox River Dr.
Grand Chute, WI 54914

Wisconsin Machine Shed
Interstate 94 & Hwy J
Pewaukee, WI 53072

Lake Country
Interstate 94 & Hwy J
Pewaukee, WI 53072

Iowa Machine Shed
11151 Hickman Road
Urbandale, IA 50322

Comfort Suites at
Living History Farms
11167 Hickman Road
Urbandale, IA 50322

Wildwood Lodge
11431 Forest Avenue
Clive, IA 50325

Sleep Inn
11187 Hickman Rd.
Urbandale, IA 50322

Iowa Trucking Co.
I-80 / Exit 284
Walcott, IA 52773

Gramma's Kitchen
I-80 / Exit 284
Walcott, IA 52773

Planted Earth Cafe
1300 River Dr.
Moline, IL 61265

Unbeatable pork dishes have been bringing folks to the Machine Shed Restaurants for years. This latest in the Machine Shed series of cookbooks introduces you to the many ways you can prepare pork for your own family.

Mary Schneckloth again takes us through the steps of creating mouth-watering pork dishes and the many accompaniments that include so much more than applesauce. The easy to follow recipes that Mary creates makes each one of us feel she is right there with us.

Mary has included a special treat. Look for the chefs hat icon. These creations are pork favorites of **The Great Chefs Of Heart Of America Restaurants And Inns.**

Notes &
Recipes

Table of Contents

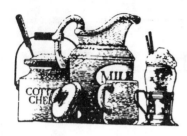

List Your Favorite Recipes Here

Recipes   **Page**

_____   _____

_____   _____

_____   _____

_____   _____

_____   _____

_____   _____

_____   _____

_____   _____

_____   _____

_____   _____

_____   _____

_____   _____

_____   _____

_____   _____

_____   _____

_____   _____

_____   _____

_____   _____

APPETIZERS

List Your
Favorite
Recipes

Recipes   **Page**

_____   _____

_____   _____

_____   _____

_____   _____

_____   _____

_____   _____

_____   _____

_____   _____

_____   _____

_____   _____

_____   _____

_____   _____

_____   _____

_____   _____

_____   _____

_____   _____

Bacon Cherry Tomatoes

8 slices cooked, drained, bacon, chopped	4 green onions, chopped
	1/2 c. mayonnaise
Salt, to taste	Cherry tomatoes

CUT thin slice from bottom of cherry tomatoes.
SCOOP out the seeds and pulp.
SALT tomato cavities and drain upside down on paper towel 20 minutes.
MIX ingredients and stuff tomatoes.
REFRIGERATE up to 2 hours.
YIELD: About 1 1/2 dozen.

Bacon Puffs

1/2 c. milk	4 slices bacon, cooked & crumbled
2 T. butter or margarine	
1/2 c. flour	1/2 c. green onion, chopped
1/2 c. shredded Cheddar cheese	1/4 tsp. garlic salt
	1/4 tsp. pepper
2 eggs	

BRING milk and butter to a boil.
ADD flour all at once, stirring constantly, until mixture forms a ball and leaves side of pan.
REMOVE from heat.
ADD eggs one at a time, stirring until mixture is smooth; add remaining ingredients.
BAKE in preheated 350° oven for 25 minutes, until puffed and golden brown.
YIELD: 3 dozen.

Appetizers

Bacon-Parmesan Cheese Ball

2 (8 oz.) pkg. cream cheese, softened
1/2 c. mayonnaise
1/3 c. grated Parmesan cheese
10 slices bacon, cooked & crumbled
1/4 c. green onions, sliced

COMBINE cream cheese, mayonnaise, and cheese in a large mixing bowl; beat at medium speed of an electric mixer until well blended. Stir in bacon and green onions; cover and chill at least 3 hours.
SHAPE mixture into a ball.
SERVE with crackers.
YIELD: 1 (4 1/2-inch) cheese ball.

Bacon-Wrapped Water Chestnuts

1 lb. sliced bacon
1 c. ketchup
3/4 c. packed brown sugar
2 (8 oz. each) cans whole water chestnuts, rinsed & drained

CUT bacon strips into thirds; wrap a strip around each water chestnut and secure with wooden picks.
PLACE in an ungreased 10x15x1-inch baking pan.
BAKE at 375° for 25 minutes, or until bacon is crisp.
MEANWHILE, in a small saucepan, combine ketchup and brown sugar; cook and stir over medium heat until sugar dissolves.
REMOVE chestnuts to paper towels; drain. Dip in ketchup mixture; place in a lightly-greased 9x13x2-inch baking pan. Spoon remaining sauce over chestnuts.
RETURN to oven for 10 minutes.
YIELD: About 5 dozen.

Cheese and Ham Nuggets

2 T. softened butter
1 c. shredded Cheddar cheese
1/2 c. all-purpose flour
1/2 tsp. paprika

1/8 tsp. salt
2 T. water
1 lb. cooked ham, cut into
1" cubes

COMBINE the first 6 ingredients; mix well with a fork.
SHAPE a thin layer of cheese mixture around each ham cube.
PLACE on a greased cookie sheet.
BAKE at 400° for 15 minutes, or until lightly browned.
YIELD: Will cover 20 (1-inch) pieces of ham.

Cream Cheese and Ham Slices

1 (8 ounce) package cream
  cheese
1 T. cream (whipping cream)
3/4 tsp. Worcestershire sauce

1/4 tsp. celery salt
6 to 10 slices boiled ham
1/4 tsp. seasoned salt
3/4 tsp. garlic salt

MIX ingredients and cream well. Spread over ham slices, roll ham slices tightly.
CHILL 1 to 2 hours.
SLICE each ham roll into 1-inch pieces.
SERVE with sprigs of parsley, strips of green and red pepper, cherry tomatoes, carrots and olives.

Crock-Pot Little Smokies

1 lg. pkg. Little Smokies
1 (12 oz.) btl. Heinz chili
  sauce
1 tsp. Worcestershire sauce

1/2 c. grape jelly
1/4 tsp. dry mustard
1/4 tsp. Italian seasoning

SIMMER on stove or in crock-pot until warm.
SERVE hot with toothpick.

Appetizers

3

Deviled Ham and Egg Appetizer

6 hard-cooked eggs
1/4 c. mayonnaise
1 T. sweet pickle relish
1/8 tsp. salt

3/4 c. finely-chopped fully-
    cooked ham
2 tsp. prepared mustard
Dash of pepper

SLICE eggs in half lengthwise. Remove yolks to a small bowl; set whites aside. Mash yolks; stir in ham, mayonnaise, relish, mustard, salt and pepper.
SPOON into the egg whites. Cover and chill until ready to serve.
YIELD: 1 dozen.

Deviled Ham Puffs

1 c. water
1/2 c. butter or margarine
1 c. flour
4 eggs
3 (4 1/2 oz.) cans deviled
    ham

1 T. horseradish
3/4 tsp. pepper
3/4 tsp. onion salt
1/3 c. sour cream

IN a saucepan, heat water and butter to a rolling boil.
STIR in flour.
STIR vigorously over low heat until mixture forms a ball, about 1 minute. Remove from heat.
BEAT in eggs, all at once, until smooth and glossy.
DROP by slightly rounded teaspoonfuls onto ungreased baking sheet.
BAKE in preheated 400° oven about 25 minutes, or until puffed, golden brown and dry.
REMOVE puff to wire rack. Cool.
MIX the rest of the ingredients; chill.
CUT tops from puffs, remove filaments of soft dough.
FILL with ham mixture; replace top.

Ham Balls

1 lb. fully-cooked ham, finely ground	1 egg, slightly beaten
	1/4 c. packed brown sugar
1 lb. ground pork	1 T. ground mustard
1 c. milk	1/2 tsp. salt
1 c. crushed corn flakes	

GLAZE:	1/4 c. vinegar
1 c. packed brown sugar	1 T. ground mustard

IN a large bowl, combine the first 8 ingredients; blend just until mixed.
SHAPE into 1-inch balls; place in a single layer in a greased 10x15x1-inch baking pan.
IN a saucepan over medium heat, combine glaze ingredients; cook and stir until sugar is dissolved.
SPOON over ham balls.
COVER and bake at 350° for 15 to 20 minutes.
UNCOVER and bake 15 to 20 minutes more, or until ham balls are just beginning to brown.
GENTLY toss in glaze.
SERVE warm.
YIELD: About 8 dozen.

Ham and Green Chilies

1 1/2 c. grated Cheddar cheese	1 1/2 c. sour cream
	1 (8 oz.) pkg. cream cheese
1/2 c. chopped green onions	1 lg. round loaf French bread,
1 (7 oz.) can green chilies	or bread of choice
1 c. diced ham	

SLICE off the tops of the loaf of bread; carve out the middle.
KEEP the top of the loaf for later, and the inside of loaf for dipping.
MIX all ingredients together and place inside the loaf; replace top.
WRAP in heavy-duty aluminum foil.
BAKE at 350° for 1 to 1 1/2 hours.

Ham-Filled Puffs

These take some time to prepare, but are really, really good.

PUFF:

1 c. water	4 eggs
1/3 c. margarine	3/4 c. shredded pizza-blend
1 c. flour	cheese
1/4 tsp. garlic powder	1/4 c. finely-chopped onion

FILLING:	1 to 2 T. dill
6 oz. soft cream cheese	4 to 5 (1/4") slices smoked ham

FOR PUFFS:
HEAT water and margarine to a rolling boil. Stir in flour and garlic powder.
STIR vigorously over low heat until mixture forms a ball, about 1 minute. Remove from heat.
BEAT in eggs, one at a time, beat until smooth. Stir in cheese and onion.

FOR FILLING:
MIX dill and cream cheese together.
SPREAD a small amount on each ham slice. Roll up and slice into small slices.
TAKE about 1/2 teaspoon of puff mixture and drop on lightly-greased cookie sheet.
PUT small slice of pinwheel ham in center of puff and place 1/2 teaspoon of puff mixture on top.
BAKE in preheated 400° oven for 25 minutes, until light and puffy.
YIELD: 2 dozen.

Appetizers

Ham Spread

1 (8 oz.) ctn. cold-pack Cheddar cheese spread, softened	1/4 c. finely-chopped green onions
	1 T. Dijon-mayonnaise blend
1 (3 oz.) pkg. cream cheese, softened	1 tsp. Worcestershire sauce
	1 tsp. prepared horseradish
1 1/2 c. minced fully-cooked ham	Party bread, crackers or
1/3 c. ground pecans	pretzels

IN a bowl, combine cheese spread and cream cheese; mix well.
Stir in next 6 ingredients.
COVER and chill at least 1 hour.
LET stand at room temperature 30 minutes before serving.
SERVE with snack bread, crackers or pretzels.

Hot Sausage Cheese Balls

1 lb. hot sausage	3 c. Bisquick baking mix
1 lb. grated sharp Cheddar cheese	

MIX all ingredients well and shape into walnut-size balls.
PLACE on greased cookie sheet.
BAKE for 20 minutes at 350°.
YOU may take these ahead of time, they will keep in the refrigerator, unbaked, for 2 to 3 days.

Lit'l Smokies and Beer

2 to 3 lb. Lit'l Smokies, (sm. sausages)	1/4 c. prepared dry mustard
	2 T. cornstarch
1/2 can beer	1 T. horseradish
1/4 c. packed brown sugar	1/4 c. vinegar

IN skillet, combine beer and Smokies; cover and simmer 10 minutes.
REMOVE Smokies from beer and put them in a crock-pot.
COMBINE cornstarch and brown sugar. Mix with beer in skillet and
STIR until mixed well.
ADD vinegar, mustard and horseradish; stir until thick and bubbly;
pour over Smokies in crock-pot.
SERVE warm.

Appetizers

Marinated Pork Tenderloin
with Sweet Horseradish

SAUCE:

1/4 c. soy sauce	1 tsp. sesame oil
1/4 c. dry sherry or Madeira wine	8 drops hot sauce
	2 cloves garlic, minced
2 T. olive oil	2 (3/4 lb.) pork tenderloins
1 T. dry mustard	1/2 c. apple cider vinegar
1 tsp. ground ginger	Party rolls of your choice

COMBINE first 8 ingredients in a shallow dish or a heavy-duty, zip-top plastic bag; add tenderloins. Cover or seal, and chill 8 hours, turning tenderloins occasionally.

REMOVE tenderloins from marinade, reserving 1/2 cup marinade; combine reserved marinade and 1/2 cup apple cider vinegar.

COOK tenderloins, covered with grill lid, over medium-hot coals about 20 minutes, or until a meat thermometer inserted into thickest portion registers 160°, turning occasionally and basting with marinade mixture during first 15 minutes of cooking time. Remove from heat; slice and serve warm or chilled, with rolls and sauce.

YIELD: 10 to 12 appetizer servings.

SAUCE:

1 c. apple jelly	1 c. pineapple-orange
1 (6 oz.) jar prepared mustard	marmalade or pineapple
1 (5 oz.) jar prepared	preserves
horseradish	1/4 tsp. pepper

BEAT apple jelly in mixing bowl at medium speed with an electric mixer until smooth. Add marmalade and remaining ingredients; beat at medium speed until blended.

COVER and chill.

YIELD: 3 cups.

Party Pitas

1 (8 oz.) pkg. cream
    cheese, softened
1/4 tsp. garlic salt
16 fresh spinach leaves
1/2 lb. thinly-sliced
    Monterey Jack cheese

1/2 c. mayonnaise
1/2 tsp. dill weed
8 mini pita breads (4")
3/4 lb. shaved, fully-cooked
    ham

COMBINE cream cheese, mayonnaise, dill and garlic salt. Cut each pita in half horizontally; spread 1 tablespoon cream cheese mixture on each cut surface.
ON 8 pita halves, layer spinach, ham and cheese. Top with remaining pita halves. Cut each pita into 4 wedges; secure with a toothpick.
YIELD: 32 pieces.

Pork Nuggets

1 c. cornflake crumbs
1 1/2 tsp. dried parsley flakes
1/2 tsp. ground mustard
1/2 tsp. onion powder
1/4 tsp. salt (opt.)
1 c. plain yogurt

3 T. sesame seeds
1/2 tsp. paprika
1/2 tsp. celery salt
1/4 tsp. lemon-pepper seasoning
1 lb. lean boneless pork, cut
    into 1" x 1 1/2" cubes

COMBINE cornflake crumbs, sesame seeds, parsley, paprika, mustard, celery salt, onion powder, lemon pepper, and salt if desired; set aside.
DIP pork cubes in yogurt, then roll in crumb mixture. Arrange pork in a single layer on a baking pan coated with nonstick cooking spray.
BAKE at 400° for 15 to 18 minutes, or until juices run clear. For a crispier coating, broil for 2 to 3 minutes after baking.
YIELD: 2 1/2 dozen.

Sausage Dip

1 1/2 lb. bulk pork sausage
2 1/2 c. chopped fresh
   mushrooms
2 med. green peppers,
   chopped
1 lg. tomato, seeded &
   chopped
1 med. red onion, chopped

1 1/2 tsp. salt
1 tsp. pepper
1 tsp. garlic powder
1/2 tsp. onion powder
2 (8 oz. each) pkg. cream
   cheese, cubed
1 c. (8 oz.) sour cream
Tortilla chips

IN a large skillet over medium heat, cook sausage until no longer pink; drain.
ADD the next 8 ingredients; cook until the vegetables are tender.
REDUCE heat to low; add cream cheese and sour cream.
COOK and stir until cheese is melted and well-blended (do not boil).
SERVE warm with tortilla chips.
YIELD: 6 cups.

Sausage-Pepperoni Loaf

Frozen bread dough
Lg., round slices pepperoni
1/2 lb. ground sausage,
  browned & drained
  on paper towel
1 1/2 T. garlic powder

8 oz. grated Italian cheese
8 to 12 oz. shredded Mozzarella
  cheese
Crushed red pepper (opt.)
1 egg

GREASE pizza pan with shortening, drop dough onto pan; cover with clean cloth.

LET rise for 1 to 2 hours, until it is double in size; then spread to pan shape.

SPREAD 1 teaspoon oil onto dough to cover; sprinkle on garlic powder and grated cheese.

BEAT 1 egg with a little water.

DROP each pepperoni slice in egg and then place them on dough until fully covered, divide sausage evenly over the top of the pepperoni. (Make sure your sausage is fully-drained and dried.)

SPREAD the Mozzarella cheese on top of all.

STARTING from the edge of pan, roll dough as a jellyroll. Shape to form as desired.

SPREAD the leftover beaten egg over dough as to glaze.

BAKE for 40 to 50 minutes, until golden brown.

YIELD: 1 loaf.

Sausage-Stuffed Mushrooms

20 to 24 lg. fresh mushrooms
2 T. finely-chopped onion
2 to 3 garlic cloves, minced
1 T. butter or margarine
1/4 lb. bulk pork sausage, cooked, crumbled & drained
3 T. Italian-seasoned dry bread crumbs
3 T. grated Parmesan cheese
1 T. dried parsley flakes
1 egg white

REMOVE mushroom stems from caps. Set caps aside (discard stems or save for another use).

IN a skillet, sauté onion and garlic in butter until tender.

COMBINE sausage, bread crumbs, cheese, parsley and egg white in a medium bowl.

STIR in onion mixture. Fill the mushroom caps; place in a lightly greased 10x15x1-inch baking pan.

BAKE at 350° for 10 to 15 minutes, or until mushrooms are tender and tops are browned.

YIELD: About 2 dozen.

Stuffed-Sausage Egg Rolls

1 lb. sausage, browned, well-drained & blotted
1 1/2 c. Cheddar cheese
1 1/2 c. Monterey Jack cheese (you may use already packaged mixed cheeses)
1 sm. can chopped black olives
1/2 c. red bell peppers, chopped
1 c. Hidden Valley Ranch dressing
1 pkg. egg rolls

PLACE egg rolls into muffin tins, grease the inside of the egg roll with vegetable oil.

BAKE at 350° for 5 minutes; remove from oven.

FILL egg rolls with sausage mixture; return to oven and bake for 5 more minutes, or until bubbly.

SERVE while hot.

YIELD: About 2 dozen, depending on how full you make the egg rolls.

Appetizers

BREAKFAST

List Your Favorite Recipes

Recipes   **Page**

_____ _____

_____ _____

_____ _____

_____ _____

_____ _____

_____ _____

_____ _____

_____ _____

_____ _____

_____ _____

_____ _____

_____ _____

_____ _____

_____ _____

_____ _____

_____ _____

Apple-Cornmeal Cakes

This recipe is one I found while traveling in Lancaster, Pennsylvania.

3/4 lb. bulk sausage	1/2 c. diced, unpeeled red
2 T. butter or margarine	apple
3/4 tsp. dried thyme	1/2 tsp. ground sage
1/4 tsp. pepper	3 c. water, divided
3/4 c. cornmeal	1 tsp. salt
2 T. all-purpose flour	Additional butter, for
Maple syrup	frying
1/2 c. chopped onion	

IN a skillet, cook the sausage and onion until sausage is no longer pink and onion is tender. Remove from skillet with a slotted spoon; set aside.

RESERVE 2 tablespoons drippings in skillet. Add butter, apple, thyme, sage and pepper to drippings; cook over low heat for 5 minutes, or until apple is tender.

REMOVE from the heat; stir in sausage and onion mixture. Set aside.

IN a heavy saucepan, bring 2 cups water to a boil.

COMBINE cornmeal, salt and remaining water; stir into boiling water. Return to a boil, stirring constantly.

REDUCE heat; cover and simmer for 1 hour, stirring occasionally.

STIR in the sausage mixture.

POUR into a greased 8x4x2-inch loaf pan.

COVER and chill 8 hours, or overnight.

SLICE 1/2-inch thick.

SPRINKLE both sides with flour.

FRY in a buttered skillet until browned on each side.

SERVE with syrup.

YIELD: 6 to 8 servings.

THE Amish in Pennsylvania have this as a staple for breakfast. For my family, it is a treat they do not get often.

Bacon-Mushroom Brunch

1/2 lb. sliced bacon, diced
3/4 lb. fresh mushrooms,
   sliced
2/3 c. green onions, sliced
12 eggs
1 1/2 c. whipping cream

1/2 tsp. salt
1/8 tsp. pepper
2 c. (8 oz.) Cheddar cheese,
   shredded
Parsley sprigs, for garnish

COOK bacon until crisp. Remove from skillet with slotted spoon; drain on paper towels. Pour off drippings, reserving 2 tablespoons.
ADD mushrooms and green onions to skillet; sauté over medium-low heat until liquid from mushrooms evaporates.
STIR in bacon; set aside to cool.
BEAT eggs until well mixed; add cream, salt and pepper.
STIR in cooled mushroom mixture.
BUTTER, or use vegetable spray, an 8x12-inch baking dish.
STIR 1 cup cheese into egg mixture; pour into prepared dish.
SPRINKLE remaining cheese over top.
BAKE at 325° for 35 to 40 minutes.
LET stand 5 minutes before serving. May garnish with parsley, cherry tomatoes, if desired.
YIELD: 8 to 12 servings.

Bacon-Sausage Breakfast

When my family stop home for Sunday breakfast, it takes this hearty casserole to satisfy them, everyone has their own dish and sometimes two. I double this. You can make whatever amount fits your needs.

1 to 2 pkg. refrigerator crescent rolls
1/2 lb. bulk sausage, cooked, drained & blotted with paper towel
3/4 c. diced onion
2 to 4 T. cooking oil
6 eggs, beaten
3/4 c. shredded Cheddar cheese

1/2 lb. bacon, cooked & crumbled
1 (4 oz.) can mushroom stems & pieces, drained
1/2 c. diced green pepper
3 c. shredded raw potatoes (may use frozen hash browns)
3/4 c. shredded Monterey Jack cheese

IN a large skillet, sauté potatoes, onion and green pepper in 2 tablespoons oil until vegetables are just tender. If necessary, you may add additional oil to prevent sticking. Remove from heat and set aside.
IN a large bowl, beat eggs, salt and pepper. Add cheeses, bacon, sausage and mushrooms; mix well. Stir in potatoes.
LINE 4 to 6 individual serving dishes with crescent roll dough, bringing dough up sides of dish.
POUR egg and meat mixture into baking dishes.
BAKE, uncovered, at 350° for 30 to 40 minutes, or until a knife inserted near center comes out clean.
LET stand 5 minutes before serving.

THIS recipe may also be made in a 9x13x2-inch baking dish.

I always serve with a fresh fruit salad, toast, jelly, peanut butter, juice, and lots of milk.

Breakfast Ham Steak and Potatoes

1 lg. baking potato	1 med. red onion
2 T. cooking oil	1 T. red wine vinegar
1/2 tsp. salt	1/8 to 1/4 tsp. pepper
1/8 tsp. dried thyme	1 ham steak, about 1/2 lb.

PEEL potato; slice lengthwise into quarters, then crosswise into 1/4-inch slices. Repeat with onion.

IN a skillet over medium heat, sauté potato and onion in oil for 2 minutes. Reduce heat; cover and cook for 10 minutes, or until potato is crisp-tender.

UNCOVER; increase heat to high. Cook and stir for 6 to 8 minutes, or until potato is browned. Sprinkle with vinegar, salt, pepper and thyme.

IN another skillet, sauté ham steak over medium heat until browned and heated through.

SERVE: Place ham on a platter and top with potato mixture.

YIELD: 2 servings.

Breakfast Sandwiches

1 T. butter or margarine	4 eggs
2 T. green onion tops, chopped	1 T. milk
1/4 tsp. salt	Dash of pepper
2 English muffins, split & toasted	8 bacon strips, cooked & drained
4 slices tomato	4 slices American cheese

MELT butter in a skillet.

BEAT eggs, onions, milk, salt and pepper; pour into skillet.

COOK and stir gently until eggs are set.

TOP each muffin half with eggs, bacon, tomato and cheese.

BROIL for 1 to 2 minutes, or until cheese melts.

YIELD: 2 servings.

Chocolate Macaroon Muffins

2 c. all-purpose flour	1/4 tsp. salt
1/2 c. sugar	1 egg, beaten
3 T. cocoa	1 c. milk
1 T. baking powder	1/3 c. vegetable oil

COMBINE first 5 ingredients in a large bowl; make a well in center of mixture.

COMBINE egg, milk and oil; add to dry ingredients, stirring until just moistened.

SPOON batter into greased muffin pans, filling 1/3-full. Spoon 2 teaspoons Macaroon Filling in center of each muffin cup; spoon remaining batter over top, filling each muffin cup 2/3-full.

BAKE at 400° for 20 minutes.

SERVE warm.

YIELD: 1 dozen.

MACAROON FILLING:	1/4 c. sweetened condensed milk
1 c. flaked coconut	1/4 tsp. almond extract

COMBINE all ingredients, mixing well.

YIELD: 1/2 cup.

Cinnamon Coffee Cake

2 c. sugar	3 tsp. baking powder
1/2 c. shortening + 1/2 stick	1 c. sour cream
margarine	1/2 c. sugar
4 eggs	3 T. cinnamon
3 c. flour	

CREAM the sugar and shortenings. Add 4 eggs; beat well.

IN a small bowl, combine flour and baking powder.

ADD to creamed mixture alternately with 1 cup sour cream.

COMBINE sugar and cinnamon.

GREASE and flour a Bundt pan.

SPRINKLE a small amount of the cinnamon and sugar mixture in bottom of pan, then a layer of batter; continue until both mixtures are used.

WITH a table knife, marble the mixture.

BAKE at 350° for 1 hour.

Danish Puff Pastry

1/2 c. butter	1 tsp. almond extract
1 c. flour	1 c. flour
2 T. water	3 eggs, beaten
Powdered sugar glaze	Chopped nuts

CUT 1/2 cup butter into 1 cup flour. Sprinkle 2 tablespoons water over mixture; mix with fork. Round into a ball; divide in half. On ungreased baking sheet, pat dough with hands into 2 strips about 12x3 inches.
IN a saucepan, heat 1/2 cup butter and 1 cup water to a rolling boil. Remove from heat immediately and stir in almond extract and 1 cup flour.
STIR vigorously over low heat until smooth.
DIVIDE in half and spread over strips on baking sheet.
BAKE about 60 minutes, until topping is crisp and nicely browned.
COOL.
FROST with powdered sugar glaze and top with nuts.

POWDERED SUGAR GLAZE:

1 1/2 c. powdered sugar	1 1/2 tsp. vanilla
2 T. soft butter	1 to 2 T. warm water

MIX all ingredients until well blended.

Egg Casserole

2 doz. eggs
1/2 c. milk
Salt & pepper, to taste
1/2 lb. cooked, diced ham
1/2 lb. cooked, crumbled
  sausage
1/2 c. green pepper, diced
1/2 c. green onions, diced

1 stick margarine
1/2 c. white cooking sherry
2 cans cream of mushroom
  soup, undiluted
3/4 c. fresh mushrooms, sliced
1 c. shredded Cheddar cheese
  (you may use other cheeses
  to suit taste)

IN a large bowl, beat eggs.
ADD milk, salt and pepper.
COOK in a large, heavy skillet with margarine, as scrambled eggs.
SET aside.
COMBINE the sherry and soup; mix well.
ADD sautéed onions and green pepper, and fresh mushrooms.
PREPARE a 9x13-inch baking dish by spraying with vegetable spray,
or greasing with margarine.
LAYER the egg mixture, meat mixture and soup mixture.
SPRINKLE the Cheddar cheese over the top.
COVER and refrigerate overnight.
TO BAKE: Remove cover and bake at 350° for 50 minutes, or until set.
YIELD: 6 to 8 servings.

English Muffin Loaves

5 1/2 to 6 c. flour	1/4 tsp. baking soda
2 pkg. active dry yeast	2 c. milk
1 T. sugar	1/2 c. water
2 tsp. salt	Cornmeal

COMBINE 3 cups flour, yeast, sugar, salt and baking soda.
HEAT liquids until very warm.
ADD to dry mixture; beat well.
STIR in enough more flour to make a stiff batter.
SPOON into two 4 1/2 x 8 1/2-inch pans that have been greased and sprinkled with cornmeal.
SPRINKLE tops with cornmeal.
COVER; let rise in warm place for 45 minutes.
BAKE at 400° for 25 minutes.
REMOVE from pans immediately and cool.

Glazed Apple Bread

1/2 c. shortening	1/4 tsp. salt
1 c. sugar	2 T. milk
1 tsp. vanilla	1 c. finely-chopped apples,
2 eggs	unpeeled
2 c. flour	1/4 c. chopped nuts
2 tsp. baking powder	1 tsp. cinnamon

CREAM shortening with sugar and vanilla until light and fluffy.
ADD eggs and beat well; sift flour, measure and sift again with baking powder and salt; add milk, apples, nuts and dry ingredients.
STIR only until flour is well dampened.
POUR batter into oiled 9x5x4-inch loaf pan.
BAKE at 350° for 50 to 60 minutes.
COOL 10 minutes and remove from pan.

GLAZE:

1/2 c. powdered sugar, sifted	1 T. water
1/2 tsp. cinnamon	2 T. butter or margarine, melted

COMBINE all ingredients and mix well.
POUR over bread, allowing to drip down the sides.
ALLOW glaze to set, and wrap tightly for better flavor.
THIS bread is best if made the day before you want to serve it.

Ham and Swiss English Muffins

2 c. (8 oz.) shredded Swiss
   cheese
1/2 c. finely-chopped green
   pepper
1/2 c. mayonnaise
1/4 tsp. salt
1 drop hot pepper sauce

1 c. diced fully-cooked ham
1 sm. onion, finely chopped
1 T. Dijon mustard
Pinch of pepper
5 English muffins, split &
   toasted

IN a bowl, combine cheese, ham, green pepper and onion.
STIR in mayonnaise, mustard, salt, pepper and hot sauce.
SPREAD 1/4 cup on each muffin half; place on an ungreased baking sheet.
BROIL 5 inches from the heat for 2 minutes, or until lightly browned and bubbly.
YIELD: 5 servings.

Hash Brown-Sausage Casserole

1 (20 oz.) pkg. refrigerated
   hash browns
1 1/4 tsp. salt, divided
1/4 tsp. pepper
1 lb. ground pork sausage
1/2 lb. chopped, cooked ham

2 stale white bread slices,
   crumbled
6 lg. eggs
1 1/2 c. milk
1 tsp. dry mustard
1 c. (4 oz.) shredded sharp
   Cheddar cheese

MIX potatoes with 1 teaspoon salt and pepper. Press on bottom and 1 1/2 inches up sides of a lightly-greased 7x11-inch baking dish.
BAKE at 350° for 10 minutes.
BROWN sausage in a large skillet, stirring until it crumbles and is no longer pink; drain.
SPRINKLE over potatoes.
WHISK eggs, milk, mustard and remaining 1/4 teaspoon salt; stir in cheese and bread.
POUR over casserole. You may refrigerate overnight.
BAKE at 350° for 35 to 40 minutes, or until set.
Yield: 6 servings.

THIS casserole would be good with a summer fruit salad, and Chocolate Macaroon Muffins.

Homemade Biscuits and Gravy

BISCUITS:
1 3/4 c. all-purpose flour
2 tsp. baking powder
1 tsp. salt

4 T. (1/2 stick) unsalted butter, cold
1/3 c. plain yogurt
1/2 c. + 2 T. milk

SIFT the flour, baking powder and salt together into a large bowl. Cut in butter until texture is the size of small peas (may use your food processor). Gradually mix in the yogurt with a fork, then the milk, until dough is soft and a little sticky.

TURN onto a lightly-floured surface and knead very briefly, only long enough to get it to hold together.

ROLL out to about 1 1/2 inches thick. Cut into 2-inch rounds.

ARRANGE on a baking sheet. (It makes the biscuits cook very well, and they do not stick if you line the baking sheet with a piece of parchment paper.)

BAKE in a preheated 425° oven for 18 to 20 minutes.

(REMEMBER that biscuits will get very "tough" if handled too much.)

SAUSAGE:
1 1/2 lb. pork sausage
1 tsp. dried sage
1/4 tsp. salt

Freshly-ground pepper, to taste
1/2 tsp. paprika
1/4 tsp. allspice

PLACE all ingredients in a large bowl; mix well.

SHAPE into 8 small patties.

PLACE in a large, heavy skillet over medium-high heat and cook until crisp, 8 minutes per side. Transfer to a platter and keep warm.

Continued on following page.

Continued from preceding page.

GRAVY:
3 T. unsalted butter, or more,
    if needed
3 T. all-purpose flour

2 1/4 c. milk
Salt & pepper, to taste
2 T. fresh sage leaves, for
    garnish

ADD enough of the butter to the skillet so the bottom is covered with 1/8-inch.

STIR, scraping up the browned bits from the bottom of the skillet.

REDUCE heat to medium and add the flour, stirring slowly until it has absorbed the butter.

COOK, stirring constantly, until it turns golden brown, at least 2 minutes.

SLOWLY pour in the milk, stirring constantly, and cook until the gravy thickens. Season with salt and pepper.

SERVE by splitting the biscuits; lay them on your individual plates and cover with the sausage patties, then the gravy, and top with a little of the fresh sage.

YIELD: 4 servings. (You will have extra biscuits. They are great with butter and jelly.)

Oatmeal Bread

1 2/3 c. boiling water	2 pkg. dry yeast
1 1/4 c. quick-cooking oats	2 eggs
1/4 c. shortening	6 to 6 1/2 c. sifted flour
1/2 c. molasses	Melted butter or margarine
1 T. salt	Small amount rolled oats
1/2 c. warm water (105° to 115°)	

COMBINE boiling water, rolled oats, shortening, molasses and salt in a large mixing bowl; cool to lukewarm.

MEASURE the 1/2 cup warm water in a mixing bowl; sprinkle in yeast. Stir to dissolve.

STIR into lukewarm oat mixture; add eggs and 3 cups flour. Beat until well blended.

MIX in enough remaining flour to form a stiff dough that is easy to handle.

DIVIDE dough in half.

FORM each half into a smooth ball; place in greased 9-inch round layer cake pan.

BRUSH tops with melted butter or margarine; sprinkle with rolled oats.

LET rise in warm (85°) place, free from draft, about 1 to 1 1/2 hours, or until double in bulk.

BAKE at 350° for 45 to 50 minutes.

REMOVE from pans.

Overnight Egg-Sausage Casserole

Your choice of bread, cut into
   1" cubes
1 c. mushrooms, chopped
2 c. shredded Monterey Jack
   cheese
6 eggs, slightly beaten

3/4 lb. bulk pork sausage
1 med. onion, chopped
1 sm. can green chilies,
   chopped
1 c. American cheese, cubed
2 c. milk or whipping cream

PLACE half of bread cubes in a greased 9x13x2-inch baking dish; set the remaining bread aside.

IN a skillet over medium heat, cook sausage and onions until meat is no longer pink and onion is tender; drain. Stir in chilies.

SPOON half of sausage mixture over bread; top with half of each cheese. Repeat layers.

IN a bowl, stir milk into beaten eggs; pour over cheese. Cover and refrigerate overnight.

REMOVE from refrigerator 1 hour before baking.

BAKE, uncovered, at 325° for 50 to 55 minutes, or until knife inserted in the center comes out clean.

LET stand 5 minutes before serving.

YIELD: 6 to 8 servings.

Sausage Gravy

1/2 lb. bulk pork sausage
1/2 lb. bulk sage sausage
1 T. chicken bouillon
   granules

Warm baking powder biscuits
1/2 lb. bulk hot pork sausage
3/4 to 1 c. all-purpose flour
5 c. milk

IN a large skillet over medium heat, cook all of the sausage until no longer pink; drain.

STIR in flour and bouillon.

GRADUALLY add milk, stirring constantly. Bring to a boil and stir for 2 minutes.

SERVE over biscuits.

YIELD: 8 to 10 servings.

Breakfast

Sausage Stroganoff

1 lb. bulk pork sausage
1/2 lb. fresh mushrooms,
   sliced
1 T. Worcestershire sauce
1/4 c. all-purpose flour
2 T. fresh parsley, minced
   (opt.)

1 med. onion, chopped
1 1/4 c. chicken broth, divided
1/4 tsp. pepper
1 c. (8 oz.) sour cream
Hot cooked noodles

IN a large skillet, cook sausage and onion until meat is no longer pink and onion is tender; drain.

ADD mushrooms; cook for 1 minute. Add 1 cup broth, Worcestershire sauce and pepper. Cover and simmer for 5 minutes.

GRADUALLY stir remaining broth into flour; mix until smooth. Stir into skillet.

BRING to a boil; boil and stir for 2 minutes. Reduce heat; add sour cream. Stir until heated through (do not boil). Add parsley, if desired.

SERVE over biscuits.

YIELD: 4 servings.

Sour Cream Pecan Tea Ring

1/2 c. margarine, melted
1 c. sour cream
1/2 c. sugar
1 1/2 tsp. salt
2 pkg. active dry yeast
3/4 c. warm water
1 egg, room temp.

5 1/2 to 6 1/2 c. unsifted flour
Melted margarine
1 c. chopped pecans
1/2 c. firmly-packed brown
 sugar
1/2 tsp. cinnamon
Powdered sugar frosting

COMBINE margarine, sour cream, sugar and salt.
DISSOLVE yeast in warm water.
ADD sour cream mixture, egg and 3 cups of flour.
Beat until smooth.
ADD more flour to make a stiff dough.
ON a floured board, knead 8 to 10 minutes.
PLACE in greased bowl; grease top.
COVER; let rise until doubled, about 1 hour and 15 minutes.
PUNCH down dough.
COVER; let rise 15 minutes.
ROLL into two 9x16-inch rectangles. Brush with margarine.
COMBINE pecans, sugar and cinnamon. Sprinkle on dough. Roll up.
Seal seams. Place in circles on greased baking pans.
SEAL ends.
CUT slits 2/3 through rings at intervals; turn sections on sides.
COVER; let rise until doubled, about 1 hour.
BAKE at 375° about 25 minutes.
FROST while warm.

Zucchini Walnut Bread

1 c. walnuts, chopped	1 1/2 tsp. salt
4 eggs	1 tsp. cinnamon
2 c. sugar	3/4 tsp. baking powder
1 c. vegetable oil	2 c. grated zucchini
3 1/2 c. flour	1 c. raisins
1 1/2 tsp. baking soda	1 tsp. vanilla

BEAT eggs, gradually add sugar, then oil.
COMBINE dry ingredients; add to first mixture alternately with zucchini. Stir in raisins, nuts and vanilla.
BAKE at 350° in 2 greased and lightly-floured loaf pans, for 55 minutes.
LET rest for 10 minutes, then turn onto a cooling rack.
GLAZE, if desired. This bread freezes very well.

Tomato with Green Chilies Eggs

1 lb. bulk pork sausage	3 T. milk or whipping cream
1 med. onion, chopped	1 (10 oz.) can diced green
1/2 lb. fresh mushrooms, diced	tomatoes with green chilies, drained
1/4 tsp. salt	1/2 c. each shredded Cheddar,
1/4 tsp. pepper	Mozzarella and Monterey
6 eggs, whipped	Jack cheeses

IN a skillet, cook sausage, onion, mushrooms, salt and pepper until meat is no longer pink. Drain and set aside.
WITH a wire whisk, blend eggs and milk for 1 minute, or until smooth.
POUR into a greased, shallow 1 1/2-quart baking dish.
BAKE at 400° for 5 minutes.
COVER with tomatoes and the sausage mixture. Sprinkle with cheeses.
REDUCE heat to 350°.
BAKE 20 minutes more, or until heated through.
YIELD: 6 to 8 servings.

Notes &
Recipes

_____

_____

_____

_____

_____

_____

_____

_____

_____

_____

_____

_____

_____

_____

_____

_____

_____

_____

_____

_____

BREADS

List Your Favorite Recipes

Recipes   **Page**

_____   _____

_____   _____

_____   _____

_____   _____

_____   _____

_____   _____

_____   _____

_____   _____

_____   _____

_____   _____

_____   _____

_____   _____

_____   _____

_____   _____

_____   _____

Aunt Jane's Batter Rolls

1 pkg. active dry yeast	1 c. milk, scalded
1/4 c. water	2 c. sifted all-purpose flour
1/2 c. shortening	1 slightly-beaten egg
1/4 c. sugar	1 1/4 c. sifted all-purpose flour
1 tsp. salt	

SOFTEN dry yeast in warm water.

COMBINE shortening, sugar and salt in a large mixing bowl. Add scalded milk; stir until shortening is melted. Cool to lukewarm.

START mixer on medium speed; add 2 cups flour.

BEAT 1 minute, or until gluten strands are practically visible. Stop the mixer.

ADD softened yeast and egg. Beat batter smooth on medium speed, about 1/2 minute.

ADD remaining 1 1/4 cups flour.

BEAT batter at medium speed until smooth, about 2 minutes. Since batter is stiff, you might need to push it away from beaters with a rubber spatula occasionally.

COVER dough and let rise until almost double, about 1 hour.

STIR down and beat thoroughly with a wooden spoon.

DROP batter by tablespoonfuls into greased muffin pans, filling them about half-full.

LET rise in warm place until double, about 30 minutes.

BAKE at 400° for about 15 minutes.

Bran Rolls

These rolls are not only healthy, they require no kneading or shaping.

1 pkg. active dry yeast	1/2 c. whole bran
1/2 c. warm water	3/4 tsp. salt
1/2 c. shortening	1 egg
1/3 c. sugar	3 c. sifted all-purpose flour

SPRINKLE yeast on warm water; stir to dissolve.

POUR boiling water over shortening in mixing bowl; stir in sugar, bran and salt.

COOL to lukewarm.

BEAT egg with rotary beater and add to bran mixture. Stir in yeast and mix well.

STIR in flour, 1/2 cup at a time.

COVER and let rise in warm place until almost doubled, about 2 1/2 hours. Punch down.

DROP dough from spoon into greased muffin-pan cups, filling cups half-full.

COVER and let rise until doubled, about 1 hour.

BAKE at 375° for 15 minutes.

YIELD: 2 dozen rolls.

Cornbread Sticks

2 c. self-rising cornmeal
1/4 tsp. baking soda
2 lg. eggs, lightly beaten
1 (10 3/4 oz.) can condensed
  golden corn soup,
  undiluted, or 1 (11 oz.)
  can corn chowder

1 1/2 c. (6 oz.) shredded
  Cheddar cheese
1 c. buttermilk
1/4 c. vegetable oil
Vegetable cooking spray

HEAT cast-iron cornstick pan at 450° for 5 minutes, or until very hot. (You may use a cast-iron skillet, and make a cornbread round, to slice into servings.)
COMBINE cornmeal and baking soda in a large bowl; make a well in the center of mixture. Combine eggs and next 4 ingredients; add to cornmeal mixture, stirring just until dry ingredients are moistened.
REMOVE pan from oven and coat with cooking spray. Spoon batter into hot pan.
BAKE at 375° for 18 to 20 minutes, or until cornbread sticks, or in round skillet, are browned. Remove from pans, and let cool slightly on a wire rack.
YIELD: 2 dozen.

Cracked Wheat Bread

2 c. cold milk
2 T. sugar
4 T. vegetable oil
2 T. salt

3 eggs
2 c. coarse rye meal
5 1/2 c. bread flour
2 pkg. active dry yeast

COMBINE all ingredients in a large mixing bowl with an electric mixer equipped with a dough hook. Blend well for about 10 minutes. Remove dough hook and allow dough to rest 20 minutes.
TURN dough out onto floured board and knead lightly into a long roll. Cut into 30 equal pieces and form into balls. Flatten slightly and place in a large, lightly-greased baking sheet.
COVER and let rise in warm place until doubled.
BAKE in a preheated 400° oven for 20 minutes, or until lightly browned.
YIELD: 30 small loaves.
SERVE warm.

Breads

Herb Rolls

1 pkg. active dry yeast	1/2 tsp. celery seed
3/4 c. warm water	1 tsp. poultry seasoning
2 1/2 c. packaged biscuit mix	

SOFTEN yeast in warm water. Stir in biscuit mix and remaining ingredients; beat vigorously (2 to 3 minutes).
TURN out on surface well dusted with biscuit mix.
KNEAD until smooth, about 25 strokes.
ROLL into a 6x14-inch rectangle, about 1/4-inch thick.
CUT dough lengthwise in thirds, then crosswise at 2-inch intervals to make 21 squares. Form each square into a ball.
IN a greased 8 x 1 1/2-inch round pan, arrange 13 rolls (not quite touching each other) around edge; arrange an inner circle of 8 rolls, leaving a 2-inch hole in center.
COVER with damp cloth.
LET rise until double (about 1 hour).
BAKE at 400° for 15 to 20 minutes, or until golden brown.
SERVE hot.

Multi-Grain English Muffin Bread

1 (1/4 oz.) pkg. active dry yeast	1/4 c. cornmeal
	1 1/4 c. warm water
1/3 c. whole wheat flour	1/3 c. quick-cooking oats
1/3 c. wheat germ	1 T. sugar
3/4 tsp. salt	2 c. all-purpose flour

IN a mixing bowl, dissolve yeast in water. Add whole wheat flour, oats, wheat germ, sugar, salt and 1 1/4 cups all-purpose flour; beat until smooth.
ADD enough remaining flour to form a soft dough. Place in a greased bowl, turning once to grease top.
COVER and let rise in a warm place until doubled in size.
PUNCH dough down (do not knead). Shape into loaf.
COAT a 9x5x3-inch loaf pan with cooking spray, sprinkle with half of the cornmeal. Place in pan and sprinkle with remaining cornmeal. Let rise to double.
BAKE at 400° for 30 minutes, or until golden brown.
YIELD: 1 loaf.

Breads

Oatmeal Bread

6 c. flour	1/3 c. water
2 1/2 tsp. salt	1 c. quick rolled oats
2 T. butter	1 tsp. sugar
2 pkg. yeast	1/2 c. molasses

POUR hot water over oats. Let stand 1/2 hour (you can do this first thing, and make your salad while the oats soak).

SOAK yeast, warm water and sugar until foamy. Add to oatmeal mixture, the salt, butter and molasses.

LAST, add yeast and flour. If dough is too sticky, add a little more flour.

LET rise to double in bulk. Punch down, and make into 2 loaves.

BAKE at 325° for 1 hour.

Onion Bread

This bread has a great beef and onion taste, that is really good with soup and a salad.

2 c. water	2 T. grated Parmesan cheese
1 (1 3/8 oz.) pkg. onion soup mix	2 T. shortening
	1 pkg. active dry yeast
2 T. sugar	1/4 c. warm water

BRING 2 cups water to boiling in saucepan; add soup mix and simmer, covered, 10 minutes. Stir in sugar, salt, cheese and shortening; cool to lukewarm.

SPRINKLE yeast on warm water in large bowl; stir to dissolve.

STIR in onion soup mixture and 2 1/2 cups flour.

BEAT with electric mixer at medium speed, scraping the bowl occasionally, 2 minutes, or by hand until batter sheets from spoon.

MIX in remaining flour, a little at a time, first with spoon and then with hands, until dough leaves the sides of bowl. Dough will be moderately stiff. Turn onto lightly-floured board.

KNEAD until dough is smooth, place in lightly-greased bowl and turn dough over to grease top.

COVER and let rise in warm place until doubled, about 1 1/2 hours.

PUNCH down, turn onto board and divide in half.

COVER and let rest 10 minutes.

SHAPE into loaves and place in 2 greased loaf bread pans.

COVER and let rise until doubled, about 1 hour.

BAKE at 400° for 30 to 40 minutes, or until browned.

YIELD: 2 loaves.

Refrigerator Potato Rolls

3 med. potatoes, mashed	1 c. scalded milk
1 sm. cake yeast dissolved in	3 beaten eggs
1/2 c. lukewarm water	3/4 c. sugar
1/2 c. shortening	2 tsp. salt
5 c. all-purpose flour	

POUR scalded milk over shortening and let cool. Then add the dissolved yeast and mashed potatoes.

ADD eggs, sugar and salt; beat well.

ADD about 4 cups of flour first, then remainder.

TOSS dough on bread board and knead well, before spreading lightly with shortening and putting back in mixing bowl.

CHILL at least 24 hours.

TAKE from refrigerator 2 hours before baking. Shape rolls or cut out with biscuit cutter.

BAKE at 400° for 10 to 15 minutes or until brown.

THESE rolls are easy and make any meal seem extra special.

Roadside Potato Bread

This bread was named years ago when Pennsylvania farmers' wives sold fresh homemade bread at roadside markets. This recipe is adjusted to today's ingredients, and utensils.

3 1/2 c. milk	2 pkg. active dry yeast
6 T. sugar	1/2 c. warm water
6 T. shortening or butter	10 to 11 c. sifted all-purpose
2 tsp. salt	flour
1/4 c. instant mashed	3 T. cornmeal
potatoes	

SCALD milk; pour into large bowl and stir in sugar, butter, salt and instant mashed potatoes. Cool to lukewarm.

ADD yeast and 4 cups flour to milk mixture.

BEAT 2 minutes with electric mixer at medium speed, or until batter is smooth. (You may beat by hand.)

MIX in just enough of remaining flour, a little at a time, first with spoon and then with your hands, to make a dough that leaves the side of bowl.

TURN onto a lightly-floured board; cover and let rest 10 to 15 minutes.

KNEAD until smooth, about 10 minutes. Place in greased bowl; turn dough over to grease top.

COVER and let rise in a warm place until doubled, 1 1/2 to 2 hours.

PUNCH down dough; cover and let rise again until doubled, about 45 minutes.

TURN onto a board and divide in 3 equal parts; round up in balls, cover and let rise 10 minutes.

GREASE 3 loaf bread pans, sprinkle bottoms and sides of pan with cornmeal (1 tablespoon to each pan).

SHAPE dough into loaves, place in pans; cover and let rise until doubled, 50 to 60 minutes.

BAKE at 375° for 45 minutes, or until loaves are golden brown and have a hollow sound when tapped with fingers.

REMOVE from pans; cool on wire racks.

YIELD: 3 loaves.

Swedish Rye Bread

1/4 c. brown sugar	1/4 c. warm water
1/4 c. light molasses	2 1/2 c. rye flour
1 T. salt	2 to 3 T. caraway seeds
2 T. shortening	3 1/2 to 4 c. sifted all-purpose
1 1/2 c. boiling water	flour
1 pkg. active dry yeast	

COMBINE brown sugar, molasses, salt and shortening in a large bowl; pour on boiling water and stir until sugar is dissolved. Cool to lukewarm.

SPRINKLE yeast on warm water; stir to dissolve.

STIR rye flour (stir before measuring) into brown sugar-molasses mixture, beating well. Stir in yeast and caraway seeds; beat until smooth.

MIX in enough all-purpose flour, a little at a time, first with a spoon and then with your hands, to make a smooth, soft dough.

TURN onto lightly-floured board; knead until satiny and elastic, about 10 minutes.

PLACE dough in lightly-greased bowl; turn dough over to grease top. Cover and let rise in warm place until dough is doubled, about 1 1/2 to 2 hours.

PUNCH down; turn dough onto lightly-floured board and divide in half. Round up dough to make 2 balls. Cover and let rest 10 minutes.

FLATTEN rounds slightly, and place on opposite corners of a greased baking sheet, instead of in loaf pans.

COVER and let rise in a warm place until almost doubled, 1 1/2 to 2 hours.

BAKE at 375° for 25 to 30 minutes, covering with a sheet of aluminum foil the last 15 minutes if loaves appear to be browning too fast.

BRUSH loaves with melted butter if you like a soft crust.

YIELD: 2 loaves.

Breads

Tomato Bread

A great sandwich bread.

2 c tomato juice	1/4 c. tomato ketchup
2 T. butter	1 pkg. active dry yeast
3 T. sugar	1/4 c. warm water
1 tsp. salt	7 c. sifted all-purpose flour

HEAT tomato juice and butter together until butter is melted. Add sugar, salt and ketchup. Let cool to lukewarm.

SPRINKLE yeast on warm water; stir to dissolve.

ADD tomato mixture and 3 cups flour to yeast. Beat with electric mixer on medium speed, scraping the bowl occasionally, 2 minutes. You may beat by hand until smooth.

MIX in enough remaining flour, a little at a time, first with spoon and then with hands, to make a soft dough that leaves the sides of the bowl.

TURN onto a lightly floured board and knead until smooth and elastic 8 to 10 minutes. Place in a lightly-greased bowl; turn dough to grease top.

COVER and let rise in warm place until doubled, 1 to 1 1/2 hours.

PUNCH down and divide in half. Cover and let rest 10 minutes.

SHAPE into loaves and place in 2 greased loaf pans.

COVER and let rise again until almost doubled, about 1 hour.

BAKE at 425° about 25 minutes, or until bread tests done.

Breads

White Bread Loaves

| 3 c. water, ice-cold | 2 pkg. quick-rise yeast |
| 7 c. bread flour, divided | 1 T. salt |

IN an electric mixer, with a dough hook, add ice water. Sift together 5 cups bread flour and quick-rise yeast. Add to ice water and mix well. Blend until a sticky dough forms.

SIFT together remaining 2 cups flour and salt; add to sticky dough mixture. Blend on medium speed for approximately 5 minutes, or until a drier dough forms. Remove from bowl and knead dough for 2 to 3 minutes.

LET dough rest for 30 minutes, covered, in a warm place.

DIVIDE dough into 7 equal pieces and knead each piece, forming into small oval or round loaves.

PLACE formed dough on a lightly-greased baking sheet and let rise until double in bulk (30 to 40 minutes).

BAKE at 400° for 30 to 40 minutes, until nicely browned.

Hints for Good Bread Making

RECOGNIZING TOP QUALITY BREAD:
If the loaf is plump and it has a tender golden crust. The crust may be crisp, but if you brush it with a little soft or melted butter while the loaf is still warm, it will be shiny and soft. Along the sides of the loaf, just below the top crust, there's an even, slight break, often called the shred. The texture is fine-grained. If you feel a slice, it should be soft and springy and a little moist.

FLOUR:
Most used is all-purpose flour, which is milled from blended soft and hard wheats. It is recommended to sift the flour before measuring, in both quick and conventional breads, to get uniform results. Whole wheat and rye flours are stirred, not sifted. Most rye flour is medium rye, this is the rye they mean in recipes.

YEAST:
Yeast is a plant; in its rapid growth it produces carbon dioxide gas, or bubbles, that causes dough to rise. Yeast grows best at room temperature of 80° to 85°. This is the ideal temperature for dough during the rising processes.

LIQUIDS:
Water, milk and potato water are the most common liquids; if using unpasteurized milk, the milk must be scalded and then cooled to lukewarm to destroy an enzyme that makes bread gummy; buttermilk does not need to be scalded.
Water produces a bread with crisp crust and wheaty flour. Bread made with milk has a more velvety grain, creamy white crumb and browner crust than bread made with water. Potato water adds a characteristic flavor and moisture to bread; it gives a loaf a little greater volume, but slightly coarser texture.

SUGAR:
Sugar contributes flavor to bread, and helps yeast to manufacture gas bubbles and the crust to brown during baking.

SALT:
Salt contributes flavor, and helps control the action of the yeast; if you use too much it checks the growth. Measuring accurately is very important, as it may throw the recipe out of balance if not measured correctly.

FAT:
Use lard, butter, margarine, vegetable shortening or salad oil, as the recipe suggests. It controls the tenderness, improves the storing quality and flavor, and aids in the browning. Fat also lubricates the gluten meshwork so the dough can expand easily.

HOW MUCH FLOUR TO ADD:
Add enough flour at mixing or kneading time to prevent the dough from sticking to your hands, keep it as soft as you can handle it. If you add flour after the dough has risen, it may make dark streaks and coarsen the texture of your bread.

TO KNEAD:
Turn dough out on lightly-floured board or other surface. Flatten it with the palms of your hands. Then pick up the edge farthest from you and fold it over to the edge nearest you. Curve your hands over the dough and push gently, but firmly, three or four times with the heel of your hands. Turn the dough a quarter of the way around, fold it over on itself again and push. Repeat this folding, turning and pushing until the dough is smooth and elastic; using a rocking-rolling motion as you knead. The dough, when kneaded enough, not only looks very smooth, but it also no longer has a sticky feel.

Breads 43

TO RISE:

The correct temperature is necessary and humidity helps dough to rise. Place dough in lightly-greased bowl; turn it over to grease the top. Cover with a sheet of waxed paper and clean towel to prevent dried crust from forming. Let rise in a warm, humid place (80° to 85°) free from drafts. An unheated oven is an ideal place. Set a pan on the lower rack, or the bottom, of oven and fill it with hot water. Another way to keep yeast dough and batter warm during rising, is to fill a large saucepan or bowl about two-thirds full of hot water. Place a wire cooling rack over the top and set the bowl of dough on the rack. In very hot weather, it may be desirable to set the bowl of dough in a pan of cool, but not cold, water. Let dough rise until doubled. To test when it is doubled, press with the tips of 2 fingers lightly and quickly, 1/2-inch into the dough. If the dent stays, the dough is doubled.

TO PUNCH DOWN:

Plunge your fist into dough to collapse it; fold edges over to center. Turn dough over in bowl. Let rise again until doubled, if recipe directs.

HOW TO SHAPE AN OBLONG LOAF:

Turn risen dough onto board; divide and let rise as recipe directs. Flatten dough with your hands. Then with a rolling pin, roll it into a rectangle the size recommended in the recipe. Starting at the narrow side farthest from you, roll tightly like a jellyroll, sealing with each turn. Seal the long seam well, then seal ends of loaf by pressing firmly with sides of hands to make a thin, sealed strip. Use care not to tear dough. Fold sealed ends under. Place loaf, seam-side down, in a greased loaf pan of the size specified in the recipe. You may lightly brush the top of the loaf with salad oil or melted butter. Cover and let rise until doubled, or until dent made by gently pressing sides of dough with finger does not disappear. Do not let bread rise too much or it may crumble, be coarse-grained and have a yeasty flavor.

EXTRA HINT:

When you get ready to shape dough into loaves, roll it with a rolling pin. This removes the big bubbles that would otherwise make holes in the bread. Pay special attention to rolling out bubbles in edges of dough.

Breads

BAKING TIPS:
Place loaves in center shelf in a preheated oven unless recipe directs you otherwise. If you are baking 2 loaves, leave at least 2 inches between pans. If you are baking 3 or 4 loaves, stagger them on 2 shelves. When you bake a large loaf, you can keep the top from browning too much by baking it on the shelf placed at the lowest oven level. You can also cover the bread loosely, if it starts to brown too fast, with aluminum foil during the last 20 minutes of baking.

For loaves with sides browned like the top and bottom crusts, use an odized aluminum (dull finish), oven-proof glass or darkened metal loaf pans. Shiny metal pans reflect the heat away from the bread. When baking in glass pans, the oven temperature needs to be 25 degrees lower than for metal. When there is no mention of the pan, other than size, it is a metal pan. The standard loaf pan sizes are (9x5x3 inches) and (8 1/2 x 4 1/2 x 2 1/2 inches).

When baking time is up, remove one loaf from pan and tap the bottom or side of the loaf with forefinger. If there is a hollow sound, the bread is done. If there is no such hollow sound, return the bread to the oven and bake 5 minutes longer, then test again.

TO COOL BREAD:
Remove the bread from pans or baking sheet as soon as baked, to prevent steam forming and making the bread soggy. Place on wire racks. Cool in a place free from drafts to prevent cracking of crust.

EXTRA HINT:
To slice warm bread, lay the hot loaf on its side on bread board. Cut in neat slices with an electric knife. If you are not using an electric knife, be sure to use a serrated knife that is very sharp.

EXTRA HINT:
When slashing or scoring the tops of loaves, as for French and some rye breads, use care not to drive out the air and flatten the loaf. Make shallow cuts with a very sharp knife or a safety razor blade.

Breads   45

Notes &
Recipes

SOUPS & STEWS

List Your Favorite Recipes

Recipes   **Page**

Baked Bean Soup

1 lb. dry navy beans	1 c. diced celery
1 1/4 lb. fully-cooked ham,	1 c. diced carrot
diced	2 tsp. chili powder
3 qt. water	2 tsp. salt
2 (8 oz.) cans tomato sauce	1 tsp. dried marjoram
1 c. diced onion	1/4 tsp. pepper

COMBINE ingredients in 6-quart Dutch oven.
COVER and bake at 350° for 4 1/2 to 5 hours, or until beans are tender.
YIELD: 14 to 18 servings.

THIS is a great meal that takes no fuss. You can make cornbread just before it's done, and serve with an equally easy dessert.

Cabbage and Sausage Soup with Rice

2 T. olive oil
1 med. onion, finely chopped
1 med. celery rib, finely
 chopped
1/3 c. parsley leaves, finely
 chopped
Salt & ground pepper, to
 taste
5 1/2 c. chicken or beef broth

2/3 c. (5 oz.) long-grain rice
2 T. butter
1 sm. carrot, finely chopped
2 garlic cloves, finely chopped
1 sm. Savoy cabbage, cored &
 thinly shredded
8 to 10 oz. fresh mild sausage
Freshly-grated Parmesan
 cheese

OVER medium-low heat, combine the oil and butter in a heavy-bottomed soup pot. When the butter melts, add the onion, carrot, celery, garlic and parsley. Gently sauté, stirring occasionally, until the vegetables are soft, about 5 minutes.

ADD the cabbage and stir until it starts to wilt, 2 to 3 minutes. Season with salt and pepper to taste and add one ladleful of the broth. Adjust the heat and simmer, covered, for about 45 minutes.

IN the meantime, prick the skins of the sausage with a fork and cook in boiling water for about 5 minutes. Allow to cool, then cut into 3/4-inch-long pieces. When the cabbage has finished cooking, place the sausages in a layer on top of the cabbage and carefully add the remaining broth.

OVER moderate heat, bring to a lively simmer, then carefully add the rice so as not to disturb the sausage. Add a little boiling water if too much of the broth has evaporated. Cook, covered, until the rice is tender, about 15 minutes.

SEASON with a grinding of pepper and 2 heaping tablespoons of Parmesan cheese. Serve with additional Parmesan cheese on the side with a fresh, hard-crusted Italian bread.

Soups & Stews

Canadian Cheese Soup

3 c. chicken broth
2 celery ribs, diced
6 oz. Canadian bacon,
trimmed & diced
1 c. milk
1/8 tsp. pepper

4 med. potatoes, peeled &
diced
1 sm. onion, diced
2 T. butter or margarine
2 T. all-purpose flour
2 c. (8 oz.) shredded Cheddar
cheese

IN a Dutch oven or soup kettle, combine the first 5 ingredients; bring
to a boil.
REDUCE heat; cover and simmer for 20 minutes or until vegetables
are very tender. With a potato masher, wash vegetables several times.
Add bacon; continue to simmer.
MEANWHILE, melt butter in a small saucepan; stir in the flour and
cook, stirring constantly. Remove from heat; add cheese and pepper.
Stir just until the cheese is melted.
YIELD: 8 servings.

THIS soup would taste great any time of the year. Top with croutons,
and sprinkle with a little Parmesan cheese, and you could serve it with
any number of combinations.

Cauliflower-Ham Chowder

2 c. sliced cauliflower
1 (13 3/4 oz.) can chicken
broth
1 c. light cream
1 can condensed cream of
potato soup

1/2 c. water
2 tsp. cornstarch
1/8 tsp. white pepper
2 c. diced, cooked ham

IN a large saucepan, cook cauliflower (covered) in chicken broth until
almost tender, about 10 minutes. Do not drain.
IN bowl, gradually stir cream into potato soup.
BLEND water, cornstarch and pepper. Stir into potato soup mixture.
Pour over cauliflower; cook and stir until thickened and bubbly.
STIR in ham.
SIMMER over low heat for 10 minutes.
YIELD: 4 to 5 servings.

Soups & Stews

49

Creamy Asparagus Soup

1 1/2 c. fresh asparagus	1 med. carrot, julienned
2 T. butter or margarine	3 sm. white onions, quartered
2 T. all-purpose flour	1 c. milk
1 c. chicken broth	1 c. cubed, fully-cooked ham
1 (2 1/2 oz.) jar sliced	1 c. half & half cream
mushrooms, drained	Salt & pepper, to taste
Grated Parmesan cheese	Chopped fresh parsley (opt.)
(opt.)	

PLACE asparagus in a saucepan with enough water to cover; cook until crisp-tender. Drain and set aside.

IN a heavy saucepan, sauté carrot in butter for 3 to 5 minutes. Add onions and sauté 2 minutes longer or until tender.

STIR in flour; gradually add milk. Bring to a boil. Boil and stir for 2 minutes.

ADD broth, ham, mushrooms and reserved asparagus. Reduce heat; add cream.

HEAT through, but do not boil. Add salt and pepper.

GARNISH with Parmesan cheese and parsley if desired.

YIELD: 4 servings.

THIS is a really great soup to make with your fresh vegetables in the summer, but equally as enjoyable in the winter with frozen or canned vegetables. My family feels they cannot eat this soup without grilled Cheddar cheese sandwiches.

Golden Stew

1 1/2 c. potatoes, peeled & diced
4 carrots, cut in 1" pieces
2 med. onions, cut in chunks
Water for vegetables
2 c. cooked ham, cubed
1 (10 oz.) pkg. frozen mixed vegetables
1 c. cream of celery soup
1 (8 oz.) jar process cheese, cut into 1" cubes

COMBINE carrots, potatoes, onions, and just enough water to cover.
COOK, covered, until tender, about 15 minutes.
ADD vegetables and ham
CONTINUE to cook 10 minutes.
DRAIN water.
STIR in soup and cheese.
HEAT for about 30 minutes.
YIELD: 4 to 6 servings.

Ham and Chicken Gumbo

6 bacon strips, cut into 1/2" pieces
2 garlic cloves, minced
1 (14 1/2 oz.) can diced tomatoes, undrained
1/4 tsp. salt
Hot cooked rice
3/4 c. chopped onion
1 c. diced, fully-cooked ham
2 c. frozen cut okra
2 c. chicken broth
1 tsp. Worcestershire sauce
8 drops hot pepper sauce
1/2 c. diced, cooked chicken

IN a large skillet, cook bacon just until crisp. Add onion and cook, stirring constantly, until bacon is crisp and onion is soft. Add garlic, ham and chicken; cook for 2 minutes, stirring constantly.
STIR in okra, tomatoes and broth; bring to a boil. Reduce heat; cover and simmer for 30 minutes.
ADD Worcestershire sauce, salt and hot pepper sauce.
SERVE over rice.
YIELD: 4 servings.

Ham and Bean Soup

3/4 lb. fully-cooked ham, cubed	3 c. chicken broth
1 med. onion, chopped	2 c. water
2 garlic cloves, minced	1 c. diced, peeled potatoes
2 T. butter	3/4 c. diced carrots
2 (16 oz.) cans Great Northern beans, rinsed & drained	3/4 c. diced celery
	1/4 tsp. pepper
	1/2 c. frozen peas
	1 T. diced parsley

SAUTÉ ham, onion and garlic in butter until onions is tender.
ADD beans, chicken broth, water, potatoes, carrots, celery and pepper; cover and simmer for 30 minutes, or until vegetables are tender.
ADD peas and cook 5 more minutes.
ADD parsley, and serve.
YIELD: 6 to 8 servings.

THIS is a great recipe to make a really tasty bean soup in a hurry.

Ham and Corn Stew

2 c. potatoes, diced	1 1/2 tsp. salt
1/2 c. carrots, diced	1/4 tsp. pepper
1/2 c. celery, diced	2 c. milk
1/4 c. onion, chopped	10 oz. Velveeta cheese, cubed
2 c. boiling water	1 regular-size can creamed corn
1/4 c. flour	3 c. cooked ham, diced
1/4 c. butter	

COMBINE the first 5 ingredients in a large, heavy saucepan; simmer 10 minutes. Leave liquid in pan and set aside.
COMBINE flour, butter, salt, pepper, milk and cheese in a 5-quart pot; stir together well, and bring to a boil for 3 to 4 minutes.
ADD the vegetables with liquid, creamed sauce, creamed corn and ham; beat through, but do not boil.
SERVE hot.
CORNBREAD goes really great with this stew.
YIELD: 6 to 8 servings.

Soups & Stews

Ham Clam Chowder

1 (14 1/2 oz.) can diced
   tomatoes, undrained
1/4 c. diced green pepper
1/4 tsp. garlic salt
1 c. diced, fully-cooked ham
1 c. water

1/2 c. diced, peeled potato
1/4 c. diced onion
1/4 tsp. chili powder
1 (1 1/2 oz.) can minced clams,
   undrained

IN a saucepan, combine the first 7 ingredients.
COVER and simmer for 25 to 30 minutes or until vegetables are tender.
ADD ham and clams; heat through.

THIS soup is good accompanied by quick and easy Beer Bread with butter, or made into a sandwich of your choice.

BEER BREAD:
3 c. self-rising flour

1 can lukewarm beer
2 T. sugar

GENTLY stir until flour is moist. Place in greased bread pan.
BAKE at 400° for 1 hour.
PUT butter on top before slicing.

Jambalaya

1 lb. boneless pork, fresh,
    diced into 1/2" cubes
3 T. vegetable oil
1/4 tsp. ground black pepper
1/4 tsp. dried thyme
1/4 tsp. garlic powder
1 (16 oz.) can tomatoes,
    crushed
4 c. water
1 1/4 c. rice, uncooked
2 chicken bouillon cubes
1 c. celery, diced
3/4 c. zucchini, diced

1 tsp. yellow chili pepper
1/4 c. scallions, chopped
1 T. parsley, chopped
1 c. ham, diced
1 c. Polish sausage, cooked &
    diced
1 c. Italian sausage, cooked &
    diced
1 c. okra, frozen, cut
1 1/2 c. sm. shrimp, cooked
1 1/2 c. onion, diced
1 c. green bell pepper, diced

IN a large saucepan, sauté pork in oil over medium heat for 15 minutes, stirring occasionally. Add pepper, thyme, garlic powder and tomatoes. Cover and cook for 15 minutes.

ADD water, rice, bouillon cubes, onions, celery, green pepper, zucchini, chili peppers, scallions and parsley. Bring to a boil. Stir to blend ingredients, cover and simmer for 10 to 15 minutes. Stir once or twice and add remaining meat ingredients. Cook for another 10 minutes and add okra and shrimp.

HEAT well and serve hot.

YIELD: 6 to 8 servings.

GREAT with fresh bread.

Soups & Stews

Navy Bean Soup

1 lb. dry navy beans	1 bay leaf
1 1/2 to 2 lb. smoked ham	2 qt. water
hocks	1 c. chopped onion
1/4 c. chopped fresh parsley,	1 1/2 tsp. salt
or 1/8 c. dried parsley	1 tsp. dried basil
1/2 tsp. dried oregano	1/2 tsp. pepper
1/4 tsp. ground nutmeg	2 c. thinly-sliced carrots
1 c. chopped celery	3/4 c. mashed potato flakes

PLACE beans and enough water to cover in a Dutch oven or soup kettle. Bring to a boil; boil for 2 minutes. Remove from heat; let stand 1 hour. Drain beans and discard liquid.

RETURN beans to kettle; add water, ham hocks, onion, parsley and seasonings. Bring to a boil. Reduce heat; cover and simmer for 1 hour or until beans are tender.

ADD carrots, celery and potato flakes; mix well.

COVER and simmer for 30 minutes or until vegetables are tender.

REMOVE bay leaf. Remove ham hocks; allow to cool. Remove meat from bones and cut into bite-size pieces.

DISCARD bones. Return meat to kettle; heat through.

YIELD: 12 to 14 servings.

THIS is good served with Jalapeño Bread.

JALAPEÑO BREAD:	1 1/2 c. grated Longhorn cheese
3 eggs	1 lg. onion, cut fine
2 1/2 c. sweet milk	1 can mild jalapeño peppers,
1/2 c. oil	drained & cut fine; remove
3 T. sugar	seeds & stems
3 c. cornbread mix	1 lg. can creamed corn

MIX all ingredients together and bake in a 9x13-inch pan at 350° until brown, about 20 minutes.

New Mexico Pork Roast Chili

I was given this recipe from a friend years ago, it is a meal in a bowl.

1 c. dry pinto beans	3 1/2 c. water
1/4 c. chopped onion	1 (4 oz.) can chopped green
1 garlic clove, minced	chilies
1 1/2 tsp. salt	1 T. chili powder
1/2 tsp. dried oregano	1 1/2 tsp. ground cumin
1 (10 1/2 oz.) bag corn chips	1 (1 1/2 lb.) boneless pork
1/4 c. sliced green onions	shoulder roast, trimmed
Shredded Cheddar cheese	Shredded lettuce
Salsa	Chopped fresh tomatoes

PLACE beans and enough water to cover in a 3-quart saucepan. Bring to a boil; boil for 2 minutes. Remove from heat; let stand 1 hour. Drain beans and discard liquid.

IN a slow-cooker, combine water, onion, chilies, garlic, chili powder, salt, cumin and oregano; Add roast and beans.

COVER and cook on high for 2 hours. Reduce heat to low and cook 6 hours longer, or until pork is very tender.

REMOVE roast and shred with a fork. Drain beans, reserving cooking liquid in a saucepan. Combine beans and meat; set aside.

SKIM and discard fat from cooking liquid; bring to a boil. Boil, uncovered, for 20 minutes or until reduced to 1 1/2 cups.

ADD meat and bean mixture; heat through.

TO SERVE, spoon meat mixture over corn chips; top with green onions, lettuce, cheese, tomatoes and salsa.

YIELD: 6 to 8 servings.

THIS can be made ahead and is a snap to serve to a crowd, they can put their own together. I also set out a container of sour cream, a dish of jalapeño peppers, and one of both red and green peppers.

I always serve cinnamon ice cream for dessert.

Soups & Stews

Pennsylvania Dumpling Stew

This is a recipe sent to me by my sister in Lancaster, PA. We have enjoyed it for many years. It is a meal in itself, all I ever serve with this stew is a favorite dessert.

1 lb. boneless pork, trimmed & cut into 1" cubes	2 T. butter or margarine
	1/2 c. chopped onion
1/2 c. chopped celery	1 clove garlic, minced
5 med. carrots	3 c. water
1 T. beef bouillon cubes	1 tsp. salt
1/4 c. all-purpose flour	1/2 c. cold water
1 (10 oz.) pkg. frozen, mixed vegetables	

DUMPLINGS:	2 T. vegetable oil
1 1/2 c. all-purpose flour	1 T. sugar
2 tsp. baking powder	1 tsp. caraway seed
1/2 tsp. salt	1/4 tsp. ground mustard
1 egg	2/3 c. milk

IN a Dutch oven or soup kettle over high heat, brown pork in butter. Add onion, celery and garlic; reduce heat to medium and cook until vegetables are tender.

CUT carrots into 2-inch pieces, then quarter lengthwise; add to pork mixture. Add water, bouillon and salt. Reduce heat; cover and simmer 45 minutes or until meat and vegetables are tender.

COMBINE flour and cold water until smooth; stir into stew. Bring to a boil; boil and stir for 2 minutes. Add mixed vegetables; reduce heat to low.

IN a bowl, combine the first 6 dumpling ingredients. Beat egg, milk and oil; add to dry ingredients all at once. Mix just until moistened.

DROP by tablespoonfuls into bubbling stew. Cover tightly and simmer for 25 minutes, or until dumplings are cooked through.

YIELD: 6 to 8 servings.

Pork Sauerbraten Stew

2 lb. boneless pork, trimmed
   & cut into 1 1/2" cubes
2 c. ketchup
2 med. potatoes, peeled &
   cubed
1 c. fresh or frozen green
   beans, cut into 1" pieces
2 celery ribs, cut into 1/2"
   slices
1/4 tsp. pepper

2 T. cooking oil
1 1/2 qt. water
1 lg. onion, chopped
3 med. carrots, cut into 1/2"
   slices
1 c. shredded cabbage
1/4 to 1/2 tsp. ground allspice
1 c. crushed gingersnaps, about
   16 cookies

IN a Dutch oven or soup kettle, brown pork in oil. Add the next 10 ingredients.

COVER and simmer for 1 1/2 hours.

STIR in gingersnap crumbs. Simmer, uncovered, for 30 minutes or until stew is thickened and pork is tender.

YIELD: 12 to 14 servings.

THIS stew would be good winter or summer, with a sandwich and a lite dessert.

Potato Soup with Italian Sausages

1 lb. Italian sausage, cut into
    1/2" rounds
1 sm. onion, in 1/2" chunks
2 lb. tomatoes, in 1" chunks
4 med. russet potatoes, in
    1/2" chunks
1/8 c. diced parsley
    (1/2 c. fresh)

2 T. chopped, fresh celery
4 c. beef or chicken stock
1 bay leaf
1/2 tsp. dried thyme
1 T. lemon juice
1/2 tsp. dried red pepper flakes
    (opt.)

BROWN sausages in a large heavy saucepan over medium-high heat, about 4 minutes.

ADD the onion and cook, stirring, until it begins to turn translucent.

ADD the remaining ingredients through the red pepper (if desired), stir and cover.

BRING to a boil.

REDUCE the heat to medium-low and simmer, covered, until the potatoes are tender and the sausage is cooked through, about 30 minutes.

STIR the soup occasionally; season with salt and pepper to taste.

YIELD: 6 servings.

Sausage Bean Chowder

1 lb. bulk pork sausage
2 (15 to 16 oz.) cans kidney
    beans, rinsed & drained
1 (28 oz.) can diced
    tomatoes, undrained
1 (32 oz.) can tomato juice
1 c. chopped onion

1 c. diced, peeled potatoes
1 c. chopped green pepper
1 tsp. seasoned salt
1/2 tsp. garlic salt
1/2 tsp. dried thyme
1/8 tsp. pepper
1 bay leaf (opt.)

IN a large soup kettle, brown sausage until no longer pink; drain well.

ADD remaining ingredients. Bring to a boil, reduce heat, cover and simmer 2 hours.

REMOVE bay leaf.

YIELD: 12 to 14 servings.

Soups & Stews

Sausage Chowder

1 lb. fully-cooked smoked
    sausage, halved & thinly
    sliced
1 med. onion, quartered &
    thinly sliced
4 c. diced potatoes
3 c. water
2 tsp. dried parsley

1 tsp. dried basil
1 tsp. salt
1/8 tsp. pepper
1 (15 1/4 oz.) can whole kernel
    corn, drained
1 (14 3/4 oz.) can cream-style
    corn
1 (12 oz.) can evaporated milk

IN a soup kettle or Dutch oven over medium heat, brown the sausage and onion. Slowly add the potatoes, water, parsley, basil, salt and pepper; bring to a boil.

REDUCE heat; cover and simmer for 15 to 20 minutes or until potatoes are tender.

ADD remaining ingredients; cook 5 to 10 minutes longer or until heated through.

YIELD: 12 servings (about 3 quarts).

Sausage-Tortellini Soup

1 lb. Italian sausage	1 c. carrots, peeled & sliced
2 cloves garlic, minced	1/2 tsp. basil
1 c. onions, chopped	1/2 tsp. oregano
5 c. beef broth	1 (8 oz.) can tomato sauce
1/2 c. water	1 1/2 c. zucchini, sliced
1/2 c. red wine	2 c. tortellini
2 c. tomatoes, chopped	1 1/2 T. dried parsley
(may use canned	1 green pepper, chopped (opt.)
tomatoes)	

BROWN sausage; drain, reserving 1 tablespoon drippings. Set sausage aside.

IN the skillet, sauté garlic and onions.

ADD beef broth, water, wine, tomatoes, carrots, basil, oregano, tomato sauce and the reserved sausage.

BRING to a boil in a 4-quart saucepan; reduce heat and simmer, uncovered, for 30 minutes. (Skim fat at this time.)

STIR in zucchini (frozen), fresh or dried tortellini, parsley and green pepper.

COVER and simmer 35 to 40 minutes.

SERVE sprinkled with Parmesan cheese and garlic Texas toast.

YIELD: 8 servings.

THIS soup is an excellent soup, and can easily be made as a creamy tortellini soup. Eliminate the green pepper, tomatoes and tomato sauce. Add 2 tablespoons all-purpose flour when you sauté the garlic and onion. Cut the beef broth down to 3 cups. Add 2 to 3 cups processed American cheese, cubed.

CHEESE-filled tortellini are excellent with this soup.

Slow-Cook Orange Pork Roast
with BBQ Beans

1 pork shoulder
1/8 tsp. pepper
1/4 c. honey
1/8 tsp. ground cloves
3 T. all-purpose flour

1/2 tsp. salt
1 (6 oz.) can frozen orange
   juice concentrate, thawed
1/8 tsp. ground nutmeg
1/4 c. cold water

SPRINKLE roast with salt and pepper; place in slow-cooker.
COMBINE orange juice concentrate, honey, cloves and nutmeg; pour over pork.
COVER and cook on high for 2 hours. Reduce heat to low and cook 6 hours longer. Remove meat to a serving platter; cover and keep warm.
SKIM and discard fat from cooking liquid; pour into a saucepan.
COMBINE flour and cold water until smooth; stir into cooking liquid.
BRING to a boil; boil and stir for 2 minutes. Serve with roast.
YIELD: 8 servings.

BARBECUED BEANS:
1 lb. dry navy beans
1 (32 oz.) btl. tomato juice
1 (8 oz.) can tomato sauce
2/3 c. packed brown sugar
2 tsp. garlic salt

1 tsp. ground mustard
1 lb. sliced bacon, cooked &
   crumbled
2 c. chopped onion
1 T. soy sauce
1 tsp. Worcestershire sauce

PLACE beans in a 3-quart saucepan; cover with water. Bring to a boil; boil for 2 minutes. Remove from the heat; let stand for 1 hour.
DRAIN beans and discard liquid.
IN a 5-quart slow-cooker, combine remaining ingredients; mix well. Add the beans.
COVER and cook on high for 2 hours. Reduce heat to low and cook 8 to 10 hours longer, or until beans are tender.
YIELD: 12 to 15 servings.

Split Pea Soup

1 1/2 c. dry split peas	2 celery ribs, chopped
1/2 lb. dry navy beans	2 med. carrots, shredded
1 lb. smoked pork shoulder	1 c. chopped onion
or picnic ham	3/4 tsp. salt
1 3/4 qt. water	1/2 tsp. pepper

PLACE peas and beans in a soup kettle; cover with water.
BRING to a boil; boil for 2 minutes.
REMOVE from the heat; let stand 1 hour.
DRAIN beans and discard liquid.
PLACE beans in a 4- to 6-quart roaster and add remaining ingredients.
COVER and bake at 350° for 3 to 5 hours, or until peas are tender and soup is thick, stirring occasionally.
REMOVE pork; allow to cool.
CUT into chunks, discarding bone and fat.
RETURN meat to the pan; heat thoroughly.
YIELD: 10 to 12 servings.

Split Pea and Ham Soup

1 lb. (about 2 c.) dry green	7 c. water
split peas	1 tsp. vegetable oil
1 tsp. salt (opt.)	2 c. diced, fully-cooked ham
2 c. chopped carrots	1 c. chopped celery
1 c. chopped onion	1 c. diced, peeled potato
1/2 tsp. garlic powder	1/2 tsp. pepper
1/4 c. chopped fresh parsley,	
or 1/8 c. dried parsley	

IN a Dutch oven or soup kettle, bring peas, water, oil, and salt, if desired, to a boil. Reduce heat, cover and simmer for 2 hours, stirring occasionally.
ADD the next 7 ingredients; cover and simmer for 30 minutes or until vegetables are tender. Stir in parsley.
YIELD: 8 to 10 servings.

Tortilla-Tomato Soup

4 slices bacon, diced
3/4 c. onion, chopped
3/4 c. celery, chopped
1/2 c. green pepper, chopped
1/8 tsp. garlic salt
1 (16 oz.) can refried beans
1/4 tsp. chili powder

2 drops bottled hot sauce (opt.)
1 (14 1/2 oz.) can chicken broth
Shredded Cheddar cheese
   (opt.)
1 to 2 med. chopped tomatoes
Tortilla chips
1/4 tsp. pepper

COOK the bacon until soft, not crispy (you may trim the excess fat from bacon if you wish).
ADD the chopped onions, celery and green pepper; stir until soft.
ADD seasonings, chicken broth and refried beans, heating through.
SERVE with shredded cheese and tortilla chips on top of soup.

Wild Rice and Ham Chowder

1/2 c. chopped onion
1/4 c. butter or margarine
1/2 tsp. salt
4 c. chicken broth
1/2 c. chopped carrots
1/2 tsp. dried thyme
3 c. wild rice
2 c. half & half cream
Minced fresh parsley
2 garlic cloves, minced

6 T. all-purpose flour
1/4 tsp. pepper
1 1/2 c. cubed, peeled potatoes
1 bay leaf
1/4 tsp. ground nutmeg
2 1/2 c. cubed, fully-cooked ham
1 (15 1/4 oz.) can whole kernel corn, drained

IN a Dutch oven or soup kettle over medium heat, sauté onion and garlic in butter until tender. Add flour, salt and pepper; stir to form a smooth paste.

GRADUALLY add broth. Bring to a boil; boil and stir for 2 minutes.

ADD potatoes, carrots, bay leaf, thyme and nutmeg; bring to a boil.

REDUCE heat; cover and simmer for 30 minutes or until vegetables are tender.

ADD rice, ham, cream and corn; heat through (do not boil). Remove bay leaf.

SPRINKLE with parsley just before serving.

YIELD: 8 to 10 servings.

YOU could use bacon in this recipe instead of ham. Sauté your bacon along with the onion and garlic. This adds a smoky taste to the soup. It is sometimes best to leave out the salt when you use the bacon.

Zucchini Soup

This soup can be made with either fresh or frozen ingredients.

1 lb. bulk Italian sausage	2 tsp. Italian seasoning
3 (28 oz.) cans diced	1 tsp. dried basil
tomatoes, undrained	1 tsp. dried oregano
3 (14 1/2 oz.) cans beef broth	1 tsp. salt
2 lb. zucchini, diced	1/2 tsp. sugar
2 med. green peppers, diced	1/4 tsp. pepper
2 c. thinly-sliced celery	1/4 tsp. garlic powder
1 c. chopped onion	

IN a soup kettle, brown and crumble sausage; drain well.

ADD tomatoes, broth, zucchini, green peppers, celery, onion and seasonings; bring to a boil.

REDUCE heat; cover and simmer for 1 1/4 to 1 1/2 hours or until vegetables are tender.

ADD macaroni; heat through.

YIELD: 14 to 16 servings.

Soups & Stews

SALADS

List Your Favorite Recipes

Recipes   **Page**

_____   _____

_____   _____

_____   _____

_____   _____

_____   _____

_____   _____

_____   _____

_____   _____

_____   _____

_____   _____

_____   _____

_____   _____

_____   _____

_____   _____

_____   _____

_____   _____

_____   _____

Bacon and Beet Salad

12 c. salad greens, you may use kale, romaine, spinach or iceberg
6 strips thick-sliced bacon, cut into 1" pieces
1/4 to 1/2 c. pickled juice (from med.-size can, reserving beets)
3 cloves garlic, minced
Salt & ground pepper, to taste
1 c. pickled beets, reserved from can, cut into 1/4" cubes
6 green onions, thinly sliced
3 hard-cooked eggs, thinly sliced

BEGIN with rinsed and dried greens, torn into bite-size pieces.
SAUTÉ bacon in a large heavy skillet over medium heat until crisp, about 5 minutes.
SLOWLY pour beet juice and stir (this will cause a lot of steam).
ADD the garlic, stir and then season with salt and pepper. Add the greens and stir to coat.
COOK, stirring constantly, just until the greens wilt and turn a darker green, 3 to 5 minutes. (Do not overcook until the greens are soft.)
REMOVE to a warmed serving platter, sprinkle with beets and onion slices. Place eggs on top, or around edges of platter. Serve.
YIELD: 6 servings.

Bacon-Broccoli Salad

10 bacon strips, cooked & crumbled
1/2 c. sunflower seeds
1/4 c. sugar
1 c. fresh broccoli florets
1/2 c. white raisins
1/2 c. mayonnaise
2 T. vinegar

IN a medium bowl, combine bacon, broccoli, raisins and sunflower seeds; set aside.
MIX together mayonnaise, sugar and vinegar; pour over broccoli mixture and toss to coat.
COVER and chill for 1 hour.
STIR before serving.
YIELD: 4 servings.

Baked Chimichanga Salad

SALSA:
3 to 4 c. chopped fresh
   tomatoes
1 to 2 jalapeño peppers,
   seeded & finely chopped

1 garlic clove, minced
1 (4 oz.) can chopped green
   chilies
1 tsp. vinegar
1/2 tsp. ground cumin

GUACAMOLE:
2 ripe avocados, peeled
   & pitted
1 1/2 tsp. lemon juice

6 to 8 drops hot pepper sauce,
   such as Tabasco sauce
1/2 c. chopped, seeded tomato
1/2 tsp. seasoned salt

FILLING:
1 c. chopped onion
1/2 c. finely-chopped celery
1 garlic clove, minced
1 tsp. salt
1/2 tsp. ground cumin
5 c. shredded or chopped,
   cooked pork
Shredded lettuce
2 c. (8 oz.) shredded Colby,
   Monterey Jack or
   Cheddar cheese

1/2 c. chopped green pepper
1 med. carrot, shredded
2 T. chili powder
1/2 tsp. dried oregano
4 T. vegetable oil, divided
1/2 c. water
20 flour tortillas
Sliced ripe olives
1 c. (8 oz.) sour cream

COMBINE all salsa ingredients; cover and chill for at least 2 hours. IN a bowl, mash the avocados. Add remaining guacamole ingredients; mix well. Cover with plastic wrap, touching surface of guacamole; chill.

Continued on following page.

Continued from preceding page.

FOR FILLING:
IN a skillet over medium heat, sauté vegetables and seasonings in 2 tablespoons oil until tender. Add pork and water; reduce heat to low and cook until water is absorbed and mixture is heated through. HEAT tortillas according to package directions. Place about 1/4 cup filling in center of each tortilla.
FOLD ends and sides over filling, then roll up.
PLACE seam-side down, on a lightly-oiled baking sheet.
BRUSH each chimichanga with remaining oil.
BAKE at 450° for 5 minutes, or until crisp and lightly browned.
TO SERVE, arrange lettuce on 10 individual plates. Top each with 2 hot chimichangas. Sprinkle with olives and cheese.
SERVE with salsa, guacamole and sour cream.
YIELD: 10 servings.

THESE may be made in advance and frozen before brushing with oil. To heat, thaw slightly. Brush with oil and bake at 400° for 10 to 15 minutes.

Salads

Basil Pasta and Ham Salad

TOMATO BASIL DRESSING:

1 c. chopped fresh tomatoes	1/4 c. chopped fresh basil
2 T. chopped green onions	2 T. olive oil
2 T. lemon juice	1 garlic clove, minced
1/2 tsp. sugar	1/4 tsp. salt (opt.)
1/4 tsp. pepper	

SALAD:

	1 (2 1/4 oz.) can sliced
2 1/2 c. (10 oz.) uncooked,	ripe olives, drained
spiral pasta	1 c. cubed, fully-cooked ham
	1/3 c. chopped fresh basil

COMBINE tomatoes, basil, onions, oil, lemon juice, garlic, sugar, pepper, and salt if desired. Chill for at least 15 minutes.
COOK pasta according to package directions until firm to the bite; drain and rinse with cold water.
TRANSFER to a salad bowl. Add ham, olives and basil; toss.
ADD dressing; toss to coat.
YIELD: 8 servings.

Broccoli Slaw

1 c. sugar	1/2 c. apple cider vinegar
1/4 c. water	1/2 tsp. mustard seeds
1/2 tsp. celery seeds	1 (16 oz.) pkg. broccoli slaw mix

COMBINE first 5 ingredients in a small saucepan; bring to a boil, stirring constantly, until sugar dissolves. Remove from heat.
POUR over broccoli slaw mix, stirring gently.
COVER and chill at least 4 hours, stirring occasionally. Serve with a slotted spoon.
YIELD: 4 to 6 servings.

Caesar Salad

1 clove garlic, crushed	3/4 tsp. Dijon mustard
1 tsp. Worcestershire sauce	1 head romaine lettuce, torn
3 T. red wine vinegar	1/2 c. croutons
1 egg	Pepper, ground
Parmesan cheese	

COMBINE crushed garlic, Worcestershire sauce, vinegar, and egg (that has been cooked in shell for 1 minute).
ADD pepper to taste, and lemon juice.
TOSS with lettuce; add croutons and sprinkle with cheese.

Crunchy Ham Salad

1 c. shredded carrots	1 c. diced celery
1/4 c. finely-chopped onion	1/2 c. mayonnaise
1 tsp. milk	1 tsp. prepared mustard
2 c. shoestring potato sticks	1 c. diced fully-cooked ham

IN a large bowl, combine carrots, celery and onion.
COMBINE mayonnaise, milk and mustard. Pour over vegetable mixture and toss to coat.
COVER and chill until ready to serve.
JUST before serving, toss in the potato sticks and ham.
YIELD: 4 to 6 servings.

Cucumbers in Sour Cream

3 lg. cucumbers	2 T. lemon juice
1 (8 oz.) ctn. sour cream	1/2 tsp. salt
1 1/2 T. dried chives	1/4 tsp. pepper

PEEL cucumbers, if desired, and thinly slice; set aside.
COMBINE sour cream and remaining ingredients into sour cream mixture; cover and chill.
YIELD: 6 servings.

Salads

71

Easy Thousand Island, Bacon Salad

2 to 3 med.-size tomatoes
1 c. thousand island dressing
1/2 c. bleu cheese, crumbled
4 slices bacon, cooked
    & crumbled

4 green onions, thinly sliced
1/2 tsp. dry basil (opt.)
1/2 tsp. oregano (opt.)

SLICE tomatoes about 1/2-inch-thick and place on either 1 serving plate, or individual salad plates.

SPRINKLE with basil and oregano, if desired.

SPOON 1 to 2 tablespoons of dressing over the tomato.

SPRINKLE with crumbled bleu cheese, divided equally between slices.

COVER with equal amounts of crumbled bacon and green onion among slices.

THIS is a really quick and handy salad for unexpected guests, or if in a hurry. (You may replace the thousand island dressing with a ranch, Italian, creamy garlic, creamy dill dressing, or any dressing of your choice.)

Fresh Mixed Greens and Parmesan Cheese

2 T. butter or margarine
1 1/2 c. chopped walnuts
1 med. head iceberg lettuce,
   torn
1/2 bunch curly endive, torn
1/4 lb. fresh spinach, torn

1/4 tsp. salt
3 T. freshly-grated Parmesan
   cheese
1 med. head leaf lettuce, torn
1/2 bunch fresh watercress, torn
1/2 c. vinegar & oil dressing

COMBINE butter and salt in 8-inch square pan.
BAKE at 350° for 2 to 3 minutes, or until butter melts. Stir in walnuts and bake 5 minutes.
SPRINKLE with cheese, tossing to coat; bake 4 to 5 additional minutes or until cheese is lightly browned.
COOL completely.
COMBINE iceberg lettuce and remaining 5 ingredients; toss gently to coat.
TOP mixture with walnuts and serve immediately.
YIELD: 12 servings.

THIS salad is really a nice salad to make when you're not sure what you want to serve with a special dish. You can experiment with this salad, using different flavored vinegars, a variety of numerous available greens, and you may try sesame seeds or any other nutmeat you prefer.

Fresh Tomato Salad

2 T. virgin olive oil
1 T. red wine vinegar
1 sm. onion, peeled & diced
3 c. yellow or orange cherry
   tomatoes, stemmed &
   halved*

1 c. loosely-packed parsley
   leaves
5 med.-size red tomatoes,
   cored & cut in 8ths
Salt & ground pepper

*YOU may have trouble finding yellow or orange cherry tomatoes; if so, just use red. You only use the others because of the color contrast.

IN a large bowl, whisk together the olive oil and vinegar. Add the onion; stir and then season to taste with salt and pepper.
MINCE the parsley, add it to the vinaigrette and mix well.
ADD the tomatoes, and toss until they are thoroughly coated with the dressing.
YIELD: 4 to 6 servings.

Garlic-Tarragon Green Salad

1 clove garlic, minced
1/4 tsp. salt
1/8 tsp. ground pepper
1/8 tsp. dry mustard

1 T. tarragon vinegar
1/4 c. vegetable oil
3 heads bibb lettuce, torn

COMBINE first 4 ingredients in a large salad bowl; mash with a fork.
ADD vinegar and oil, blending well. Add lettuce; toss gently.
YIELD: 4 to 6 servings.

Salads

Green Bean-Spinach Salad
with Bacon Vinaigrette

1/2 c. green beans, blanched, & cooled

2 sm. red potatoes, cooked & quartered

2 c. fresh spinach, washed, drained & patted dry (you may add 1/2 c. radicchio, if desired)

1/4 c. mushrooms, sliced

1/4 c. bean sprouts

1 c. cooked ham, cut into strips

1 tsp. olive oil

Salt & pepper, to taste

PLACE prepared spinach on a dinner plate.

ARRANGE blanched green beans, quartered potatoes and mushroom slices around rim of plate.

SPRINKLE sprouts over entire salad.

PLACE ham strips on top of salad, sprinkle with olive oil.

SERVE with bacon vinaigrette.

BACON VINAIGRETTE DRESSING:

Use any vinaigrette dressing you choose

1 c. water

1/4 c. bacon bits

3 T. sugar

2 tsp. cornstarch, mixed with 1 tsp. water

IN a small saucepan, combine your choice of vinaigrette dressing, water, bacon bits and sugar.

BRING to a boil and reduce heat.

WHISK in cornstarch mixed with water, and simmer until sauce thickens.

COOL slightly, and refrigerate; allow to cool completely before using on salad.

Salads

Grilled Tenderloin Salad

DRESSING:
1/2 c. orange juice
2 T. cider vinegar
2 tsp. honey

1/2 tsp. coarsely-ground pepper
2 T. olive oil
1 T. grated orange peel
2 tsp. Dijon mustard

SALAD:
1 pork tenderloin (1 lb.),
  trimmed
1/4 c. chopped pistachios
  or cashews (opt.)

10 c. torn salad greens
2 seedless oranges, peeled &
  sliced

IN a small bowl, combine all dressing ingredients; cover and chill.
GRILL pork, covered, over medium coals for 15 to 20 minutes or until
meat thermometer reads 160° to 170°, turning occasionally. Let stand
for 5 minutes; thinly slice tenderloin.
TO SERVE, line a large platter with greens; top with orange sections
and tenderloin. Sprinkle with nuts, if desired. Drizzle with dressing.
YIELD: 5 servings.

Layered Lettuce Salad

SALAD:
1/2 head lettuce, torn &
  dried
1 c. celery, diced
2 green onions, thinly sliced

1/2 c. green pepper, diced
1/2 carrot, grated
1/4 c. thinly-sliced radishes
1 (16 oz.) pkg. frozen peas,
  uncooked

DRESSING:
2 c. Hellmann's real
  mayonnaise

1 tsp. sugar
1/2 tsp. lemon juice

TOPPING:
1 (8 oz.) pkg. shredded
  Cheddar cheese

6 slices bacon, fried &
  crumbled

IN a deep serving dish, place all ingredients in order given, beginning
with lettuce and ending with peas; mix mayonnaise, sugar and lemon
juice, and spread over peas.
SPRINKLE cheese and bacon on top.
DO not mix!
COVER tightly and refrigerate overnight.

Salads

Mandarin Salad

1 med. head bibb or Boston lettuce, torn	1 ripe avocado, peeled & thinly sliced
1 (11 oz.) can mandarin oranges, chilled & drained	2 green onions, thinly sliced Freshly-ground pepper, to taste
1/2 c. coarsely-chopped pecans	1/3 c. Italian dressing

COMBINE first 6 ingredients in a salad bowl.
ADD the Italian dressing just before serving, and toss gently.
YIELD: 4 servings.

Mandarin Orange and Lettuce Salad

6 c. torn mixed greens, or 1 (16 oz.) pkg. mixed lettuces	1 (2 oz.) pkg. cashew nuts, toasted (1/3 c.)
1 (11 oz.) can mandarin oranges, drained	1/2 c. commercial Italian salad dressing or sweet-sour salad dressing
1/3 c. golden raisins	

COMBINE first 4 ingredients in a salad bowl.
POUR salad dressing over salad, and toss.
SERVE immediately.
YIELD: 4 servings. You may increase the size of this recipe, depending on the number of dinners you are serving.

Pork Salad

1 lb. pork from roast, diced	1/4 c. celery, diced
1/2 c. mayonnaise	1/2 tsp. spicy brown or Dijon mustard
1 apple, peeled, cored & diced	Salt & pepper, to taste
1 T. apple juice	Pineapple spears

MIX pork, mayonnaise, apple, apple juice, celery and mustard; season with salt and pepper.
CHILL 1 hour.
SERVE with fresh pineapple spears or other fruit of choice.
YIELD: 4 servings.

Red Cabbage and Apple Slaw

7 c. finely-shredded red
  cabbage
1/3 c. cider vinegar
2 tsp. olive oil
1 tsp. Dijon mustard
1/4 tsp. pepper

8 red cabbage leaves (opt.)
1 1/2 c. diced Golden Delicious
  apple
1 tsp. sugar
1/4 tsp. salt
1/2 tsp. caraway seeds (opt.)

COMBINE CABBAGE AND APPLE; set aside.
COMBINE vinegar and next 5 ingredients in a jar; add caraway seeds,
if desired. Cover tightly and shake vigorously.
DRIZZLE over cabbage; toss gently. Cover and chill thoroughly.
Serve on red cabbage leaves, if desired.
YIELD: 8 servings.

Romano Cheese and Bacon Salad

About 6 c. romaine
  lettuce, cut in 1" strips
4 med.-size tomatoes,
  cut into wedges
2 to 3 green onions, thinly
  sliced

8 oz. Romano cheese
Croutons (opt.)
Salt, to taste
1 lg. garlic clove, peeled
2 tsp. olive oil

DRESSING:
3 oz. olive oil
Juice of 1 lemon
1/2 tsp. oregano

1/2 tsp. mint leaves
Ground black pepper, to taste
Raw egg

RUB salad bowl with salt, garlic clove and 2 teaspoons oil; add tomato
wedges, green onions and lettuce.
COVER with Romano cheese.
MIX dressing ingredients and place in a blender until smooth.
POUR over salad; marinate at least 1 hour.
TOSS, and add croutons, if desired.

Salads

Sauerkraut Salad

2 c. sauerkraut, drained
1/2 c. sugar
1/2 c. celery, finely diced

1/2 c. green pepper, finely
  diced
1/2 c. carrots, finely diced
1/4 c. onion, finely diced

COMBINE all ingredients.
PLACE in container and refrigerate at least 24 hours before serving.
WILL keep in refrigerator for up to 2 weeks.

Spinach-Apple Salad

4 slices bacon
4 c. tightly-packed fresh
  spinach, trimmed &
  torn into bite-size pieces
Freshly-ground pepper
1/3 c. mayonnaise

1/4 c. frozen orange juice
  concentrate, thawed &
  undiluted
1 lg. Red Delicious apple,
  unpeeled, cored & thinly
  sliced

PLACE bacon on a microwave-safe rack in a baking dish; cover with paper towels. Microwave on High 3 to 4 minutes, or until crisp. Crumble bacon, and set aside.
COMBINE spinach, apple and bacon in a large bowl. Combine mayonnaise and orange juice concentrate. Add to spinach mixture; toss gently.
SPRINKLE with pepper.
YIELD: 4 servings.

Spinach-Apricot Salad

1 c. boiling water
1 lb. fresh spinach
3 T. apricot preserves
3/4 c. coarsely-chopped
    macadamia nuts, toasted

1 (6 oz.) pkg. dried apricot
    halves
3 T. cider vinegar
1/2 c. vegetable oil

POUR boiling water over apricots; let stand 30 minutes. Drain well and set aside.
REMOVE stems from spinach; wash leaves thoroughly, and pat dry. Tear into bite-size pieces; set aside.
COMBINE vinegar and preserves in container of an electric blender; process until smooth, stopping once to scrape down sides. With blender on high, gradually add oil in a slow, steady stream.
COMBINE spinach, half of apricot halves, half of nuts, and dressing; toss gently. Sprinkle with remaining apricot halves and nuts. Serve immediately.
YIELD: 8 servings.

Spinach Salad

10 oz. fresh spinach, may
    use romaine or iceberg
    lettuce
6 slices fried & crumbled
    bacon
6 green onions, thinly sliced
1 c. thinly-sliced mushrooms

2 T. lemon juice
6 T. olive oil
3/4 tsp. salt
1/8 tsp. pepper
1 garlic clove, minced
1/4 tsp. sugar
1 egg yolk

BEGIN with washed, drained and dried greens. Sprinkle crumbled bacon over spinach; follow with sliced mushrooms and green onions. CHILL.
COMBINE remaining ingredients and blend well; chill.
TOSS just before serving.

Spinach Salad with Rice

1 c. long-grain rice,	1/2 c. Italian dressing
uncooked	1/2 tsp. sugar
1 T. soy sauce	1/2 c. sliced celery
2 c. shredded fresh spinach	6 slices bacon, cooked &
1/2 c. sliced green onions	crumbled

COOK rice according to package directions; rinse and drain; set aside.
COMBINE dressing, soy sauce and sugar in a large bowl. Stir in rice.
Cover and chill 2 hours.
STIR spinach and remaining 3 ingredients into rice mixture. Serve immediately.
YIELD: 6 to 8 servings.

Stuffed Apple Salad

2 to 3 Red Delicious apples	Pineapple juice or lemon juice
1 (8 oz.) pkg. cream cheese,	2 to 3 T. honey
softened	1/3 c. finely-chopped dates
1/4 c. chopped pecans	Lettuce leaves

CORE unpeeled apples and cut into 3/4-inch-thick rings; dip in pineapple juice to prevent browning; set aside.
PLACE cream cheese in a small mixing bowl; beat at medium speed with an electric mixer until smooth. Add honey; beat at medium speed until light and fluffy.
STIR in dates and pecans.
ARRANGE apple rings on lettuce leaves. Pipe or dollop cream cheese mixture into center of each apple ring.
YIELD: 6 servings.

Summer Fruit Salad

1 fresh pineapple, peeled,
   cored & cubed
1 qt. fresh, hulled strawberries
1/2 c. fresh or frozen
   blueberries, thawed
1/2 c. fresh or frozen
   raspberries, thawed

1 (11 oz.) can mandarin
   oranges, drained
2 c. orange juice
1/2 c. sugar
1/4 c. cream sherry
1/2 tsp. almond extract
1/2 tsp. vanilla extract

COMBINE first 5 ingredients in a large bowl.
COMBINE remaining ingredients, stirring until sugar dissolves.
POUR sherry mixture over fruit mixture, tossing lightly.
COVER and chill 2 to 3 hours.
YIELD: 10 servings.

Sweet Coleslaw

1 (10 oz.) pkg. finely-
   shredded cabbage (6 c.)
2 lg. carrots, scraped &
   shredded
1/2 tsp. salt

1/4 tsp. pepper
1/2 c. salad dressing or
   mayonnaise
2 T. sugar

(YOU may also use commercial coleslaw dressing.)
COMBINE cabbage and carrot in a large bowl. Sprinkle with sugar, salt and pepper; toss gently. Stir in salad dressing.
COVER and chill, if desired.
YIELD: 3 to 4 servings.

Vegetable-Cheese Frozen Salad

1 (3 1/4 oz.) pkg. regular
  lemon pudding mix
2 beaten eggs
1 (20 oz.) can crushed
  pineapple, drained

1/2 c. bleu cheese salad
  dressing
1/4 c. finely-chopped green
  pepper
Lettuce leaves

PREPARE pudding according to directions, substituting 2 eggs for the 2 egg yolks. Cover with a clear plastic wrap to prevent skin from forming. Cool 20 minutes.

STIR occasionally and re-cover. Stir in pineapple and green pepper.

TURN into a 9x9x2-inch pan which has been buttered or sprayed with a vegetable spray. Cover and freeze.

REMOVE from freezer 10 minutes before serving. Cut into squares and serve on lettuce leaf; garnish with a green pepper ring.

YIELD: 9 servings.

Wilted Lettuce-Bacon Salad

8 c. mixed greens, rinsed dried & torn	1 lg. clove garlic, peeled & minced
2 c. green onions, trimmed & cut into thin rounds	2 T. red wine vinegar
6 slices thick-sliced bacon, cut into 1" pieces	2 T. water
	1 tsp. lightly-packed brown sugar
	Salt & pepper, to taste

PLACE greens and green onions in a large heatproof salad bowl. Toss well, and set aside.

FRY bacon in a medium-size heavy skillet over medium-high heat until crisp, 5 minutes.

STIR in garlic, then deglaze pan with the vinegar and water, stirring constantly. (This will smoke quite a bit.)

ADD the brown sugar and stir. Season to taste with salt and pepper.

POUR dressing over the salad greens, and toss until they are thoroughly coated.

SERVE immediately.

YIELD: 4 servings.

THIS was the first salad we would have in the summer, the second the lettuce, kale, etc. were ready. It's still my first thought of spring salad; later into the summer, when the broccoli is ready, it is really good with this salad.

VEGETABLES

List Your Favorite Recipes

Recipes   **Page**

_____   _____

_____   _____

_____   _____

_____   _____

_____   _____

_____   _____

_____   _____

_____   _____

_____   _____

_____   _____

_____   _____

_____   _____

_____   _____

_____   _____

_____   _____

Bacon and Cheese Potatoes

4 med. potatoes, peeled & diced	1/2 lb. sliced bacon, cooked & crumbled
1 c. diced processed American cheese	3/4 c. mayonnaise
	1/4 c. sliced stuffed olives
2 T. chopped onion	2 T. chopped green pepper

IN a saucepan, cook potatoes in water until tender; drain.
STIR in remaining ingredients. Spoon into an ungreased 8-inch square baking dish.
BAKE, uncovered, at 350° for 30 minutes, or until bubbly and heated through.
YIELD: 6 to 8 servings.

Bacon-Onion Pie

1 prebaked 8" pie pastry	Salt & pepper, to taste
2 med. onions, peeled & thinly sliced	1/4 c. whipping cream
	6 slices thick-sliced bacon

PLACE 1/2 of the onions in prebaked pastry; season with salt and pepper.
REPEAT with the remaining onions.
POUR the cream over the onions; arrange bacon slices over top, overlapping, if necessary.
BAKE in a preheated 350° oven for about 55 minutes.
COOL for 5 minutes before serving.

Beer-Batter Potatoes

1 c. flour	2 eggs, separated
1 tsp. paprika	3/4 can beer
1 tsp. pepper	Crumbs of your choice
1 T. salt	(cracker, cornflake,
2 T. butter, melted	cornmeal, etc.)

MIX flour, paprika, pepper, salt and melted butter.
ADD egg yolks; mix well.
ADD 3/4 can of beer to flour mixture; mix well. Allow mixture to stand 1 hour.
BEAT egg whites until stiff. Then fold the stiffly-beaten egg whites into the beer mixture.
LET stand 30 minutes.
PREPARE large Idaho baking potatoes. Prick the skin in the usual manner before coating the potatoes. Coat potatoes with the beer batter and then roll in crumbs of choice.
BAKE the potatoes at 400° for 45 minutes to 1 hour, depending on the size of the potatoes. (If needed, you may add the remaining 1/4 can of beer.)
THIS mixture may also be used for onion rings.

ANOTHER VARIATION:

1 1/2 c. flour	Salt & pepper, to taste
1 can beer	

BAKE potatoes until nearly done. Then dip them in beer batter and roll in fine cracker crumbs.
DEEP fry until brown.
RETURN to the oven another 15 to 20 minutes, or until tender.

Carrot Casserole

1 lg. bag carrots	French-fried onion rings,
1/2 can evaporated milk	canned or frozen
1 can Cheddar cheese soup	

BOIL carrots and slice. Place in buttered casserole.
MIX cheese soup and milk. Place in casserole in layers of carrots and soup mixture. Top with onions.
BAKE at 350° for 30 minutes, or until bubbly.

Vegetables

Cheese Potatoes

3 T. butter or margarine
1 tsp. salt
1/4 tsp. pepper
1 c. (8 oz.) shredded
  Cheddar cheese

6 lg. potatoes, peeled & thinly
  sliced
1 c. milk
Chopped parsley

MELT butter in a large nonstick skillet. Cook potatoes until almost tender and lightly browned. Sprinkle with salt and pepper. Pour milk over all; boil gently until milk is absorbed. Sprinkle with cheese and allow to melt. Stir. Sprinkle with parsley and serve immediately.
YIELD: 6 servings.

Cinnamon Beans with Bacon

1 T. butter
1/4 tsp. ground cinnamon
1/2 c. chicken broth
Dash of ground pepper
6 slices bacon, fried crisp &
  crumbled

1/4 c. chopped onion
1 1/2 lb. fresh green beans
  (may use frozen)
1/8 tsp. salt
2 T. tomato paste

IN a medium saucepan, melt butter and sauté onion with cinnamon until onion is transparent.
STIR in green beans, chicken broth, salt and pepper.
HEAT to boiling; reduce heat and simmer 20 minutes, or until beans are tender.
GENTLY mix in tomato paste and bacon. Serve immediately.
YIELD: 6 servings.

Dirty Rice

This recipe appeared in the Leader some time ago, and I really like to use it as a side vegetable.

1 tsp. salt	1 lb. ground pork
1/2 tsp. black pepper	1 med. onion, chopped
1 tsp. dry mustard	1 med. bell pepper, chopped
1/2 tsp. thyme leaves	3 cloves garlic, minced
1 1/4 tsp. paprika	2 T. fresh, or 1 T. dry parsley
1 tsp. cumin	1 T. butter
1/2 tsp. oregano	2 c. chicken stock
2 T. vegetable oil	2 c. uncooked converted rice
2 bay leaves	2 green onions, chopped

COMBINE all seasonings in a small bowl and set aside.
WARM a large skillet; add oil and bay leaves. Heat for 1 minute.
ADD ground pork and cook until browned. Drain excess grease.
ADD seasonings and blend well.
ADD onions, bell pepper, garlic and parsley.
COOK 5 minutes, or until vegetables are soft.
ADD butter and stir until melted.
ADD chicken stock, then rice; mix thoroughly.
Add green onions and cook, covered, 20 to 25 minutes.
YIELD: 8 servings.

Eggplant Stuffed with Pork Dressing

1 lg. eggplant (1 1/2 lb.)
1 egg
1/2 c. grated Parmesan or
   Romano cheese
1 1/2 tsp. dried oregano
1/2 tsp. pepper

1 lb. ground pork
1/2 c. dry bread crumbs
1/4 c. fresh parsley, or 1/8 c.
   dried parsley
1/2 tsp. salt
1 (15 oz.) can tomato sauce

CUT off stem of eggplant; cut eggplant in half lengthwise. Scoop out and reserve center, leaving a 1/2-inch shell.
STEAM shells for 3 to 5 minutes, or just until tender; drain. Cube reserved eggplant.
IN a saucepan, cook eggplant cubes in boiling water for 6 to 8 minutes, or just until tender; drain and set aside.
IN a skillet over medium heat, cook pork until no longer pink; drain.
ADD eggplant cubes, egg, bread crumbs, cheese, parsley, oregano, salt and pepper; mix well.
FILL shells; place in a greased 9-inch square baking dish. Pour tomato sauce over eggplant.
COVER and bake at 350° for 25 to 30 minutes, or until heated through.
YIELD: 4 servings.

French-Fried Cauliflower - Au Gratin

1 sm. head cauliflower	2 1/2 c. fine cracker crumbs
2 eggs	Vegetable oil
2 T. water	Cheddar cheese sauce

REMOVE large outer leaves of cauliflower. Break cauliflower into flowerets.

COOK, covered, in a small amount of boiling, salted water; beat well.

DREDGE flowerets in cracker crumbs, then dip in egg.

DREDGE again in cracker crumbs.

DEEP FRY in hot oil (375°) until golden brown.

DRAIN on paper towels; serve with Cheddar Cheese Sauce (see below).

YIELD: 4 to 6 servings.

CHEDDAR CHEESE SAUCE:

2 T. butter or margarine	2 T. all-purpose flour
1 c. milk	1/4 tsp. salt
Dash of white pepper	

MICROWAVE DIRECTIONS: Place butter in a 1-quart measure. Microwave on High for 45 seconds, or until melted.

ADD flour, stirring well. Microwave at High for 3 to 4 minutes, or until thickened and bubbly, stirring after 2 minutes, then at 1-minute intervals.

STIR in 1 cup (4 ounces) shredded Cheddar cheese and 1/4 teaspoon dry mustard with salt and pepper.

Vegetables

Grandma Herbert's Bacon-Green Beans

1 lb. fresh green beans,
stemmed & cut in 2" to
4" pieces
2/3 to 1 c. water

4 strips thick-sliced bacon,
cut into 1/2" pieces
Salt & pepper, to taste

PLACE all ingredients together in a medium-size saucepan over medium-high heat.

COVER and bring to a boil; reduce heat to low and cook for about 45 minutes, or until beans have turned a darker, more olive green and are tender.

STIR occasionally.

REMOVE cover and cook an additional 20 to 25 minutes, or until liquid has evaporated.

SERVE immediately.

Lima Bean Casserole

1/2 lb. bulk sage pork sausage
2 med. carrots, thinly sliced
1/2 c. water
1/4 tsp. salt

2 (10 oz.) pkg. frozen lima
beans
1/2 tsp. sugar
Pinch of pepper

IN a saucepan, cook and crumble sausage until no longer pink; drain.

ADD lima beans, carrots, water, sugar, salt and pepper.

COOK, uncovered, for 20 to 25 minutes, or until vegetables are tender; drain.

YIELD: 10 servings.

Vegetables

Marinated Vegetables

1 c. cauliflower, cut in 1"
  cubes
1 c. carrots, sliced
1 c. broccoli florets
1/2 c. red bell pepper, cut in
  thin strips

1/2 c. green bell pepper, cut in
  thin strips
1 (10 oz.) can kidney beans,
  drained & rinsed
2 c. Italian dressing (may use
  light)

BLANCH cauliflower, carrots and broccoli in boiling, salted water
until almost done.
DRAIN and allow to steam-dry in a colander.
COOL slightly and mix with remaining ingredients.
REFRIGERATE for at least 2 hours.
MIX well, and serve on a bed of lettuce.

New Potatoes

1 lb. sm. new potatoes,
  peeled
2 T. bacon drippings
1/4 tsp. salt

1/4 tsp. pepper
1 T. melted butter or margarine
1 T. fresh parsley (1 1/2 tsp.
  dry)

COOK potatoes in boiling water to cover until tender; drain.
HEAT bacon drippings in a heavy ovenproof skillet over medium
heat. Add potatoes and cook 10 minutes or until lightly browned,
turning frequently. Sprinkle with salt and pepper.
BAKE at 400° for 30 minutes or until browned, turning once. Stir in
melted butter, and sprinkle with parsley, if desired.
YIELD: 3 to 4 servings.

Pork Tenderloin and Baked Potatoes

1 lb. pork tenderloin, cut 1/2"
   thick, across the grain,
   in thin strips
4 lg. baking potatoes
Vegetable oil
2 T. butter

1 T. Dijon mustard
1/2 c. coarsely-chopped onion
1 sm. green pepper, coarsely
   chopped
1/3 c. half & half
1/2 c. shredded Swiss cheese

SCRUB potatoes; prick each with a fork in several places.
RUB skins lightly with oil.
BAKE at 375° for 50 to 60 minutes, or until tender.
MEANWHILE, melt butter in large skillet over medium-high heat.
Add green pepper and onion.
COOK and stir 2 minutes; remove.
ADD pork tenderloin, 1/3 at a time, cooking and stirring 3 to 4 minutes.
RETURN pepper and onion to pan.
SEASON with salt and pepper, if desired; keep warm.
PLACE half & half in small saucepan; stir in cheese and mustard.
COOK and stir over medium heat until cheese is melted.
CUT potatoes lengthwise across the top; gently push ends to open and break up pulp.
SPOON equal amounts of pork mixture into each potato; top with an equal amount of cheese sauce.
YIELD: 4 servings.

Scalloped Potatoes, Bacon and Cheese

4 lb. russet potatoes, peeled
   & quartered
1 garlic cloves, peeled &
   cut in half
6 slices thick-sliced bacon,
   cut into 1/2" pieces

2 c. milk
1/2 c. whipping cream
Salt & pepper, to taste
2 oz. American cheese
2 oz. Cheddar cheese, sharp

RUB garlic halves on the bottom and sides of a 9x13-inch baking dish.
COOK the potatoes until nearly cooked, but firm in the center, about 15 minutes.
SAUTÉ bacon in a heavy skillet just until golden (do not fry until crisp). Remove bacon from skillet and set aside. Reserve pan drippings.
GRATE the potatoes into prepared baking dish, using larger holes of grater.
SEASON with salt and pepper; sprinkle with half the bacon and 2 teaspoons of pan drippings.
REPEAT with remaining potatoes, bacon and reserved pan drippings.
COMBINE the milk and cream; pour over the potatoes. Sprinkle with the cheeses.
COVER with foil and bake in preheated 350° oven for 25 minutes.
REMOVE the foil and bake an additional 20 minutes, or until cheese has melted.
REMOVE from oven and let stand 5 minutes before serving.
YIELD: 6 to 8 servings.

THIS makes a great side-dish with any meal.

Sesame Green Beans and Asparagus

1/4 lb. green beans, cut in
   half, or 2" long
1/4 lb. asparagus, cut in 2"
   lengths
1 T. dry sherry

1 tsp. soy sauce
2 T. chicken broth
1 T. sesame seeds, toasted
1 tsp. sesame oil

IN a heavy skillet or wok, heat sesame oil. Quickly sauté green beans and asparagus until skins wrinkle.
ADD sherry, soy sauce and chicken stock; simmer until tender.
TOSS with toasted sesame seeds and serve.
YIELD: 6 servings.

Vegetables

Stir-Fried Squash

3 T. vegetable oil	1 clove garlic, crushed
3/4 lb. zucchini, sliced	1 c. diced tomatoes
3/4 lb. yellow squash, sliced	1 T. Worcestershire sauce
1/2 c. chopped onion	2 T. tomato paste
1 tsp. salt	

POUR oil into preheated wok or heavy skillet; allow to heat to medium. Add squash, onion and garlic; stir-fry 2 minutes.
ADD remaining ingredients; simmer 8 to 10 minutes, or until vegetables are crisp-tender, stirring occasionally.
YIELD: 6 servings.

Sunshine Carrots

5 (or more) med.-size carrots	1/4 tsp. salt
	1/4 tsp. ginger
1 T. sugar	1/4 c. orange juice
1/4 tsp. cornstarch	2 T. butter

CUT carrots in 1/4-inch slices diagonally, and cook.
COMBINE sugar, cornstarch, salt, ginger and orange juice.
COOK, stirring constantly; boil 1 minute. Add 2 tablespoons butter and stir.
POUR over hot carrots.
TOSS to coat evenly.
YIELD: 4 servings.

Vegetables   95

Whipped Potatoes

2 1/2 lb. potatoes, peeled,
quartered & cooked
1 (3 oz.) pkg. cream cheese,
softened
1/4 c. butter or margarine,
softened
1/2 to 3/4 c. sour cream
Paprika (opt.)
Salt & pepper, to taste
1/2 tsp. garlic salt

IN a large bowl, mash the potatoes. Add the cream cheese, sour cream, garlic salt, butter and pepper; mix until smooth.
TRANSFER to a greased 1 1/2-quart baking dish. Sprinkle with paprika if desired.
BAKE, uncovered, at 350° for 30 minutes or until heated through.
YIELD: 6 to 8 servings.

Zesty Broccoli Spears

1 lb. fresh broccoli
3 T. lemon juice
1/8 tsp. pepper
3 T. olive oil
1/4 tsp. salt
1 med. garlic clove, crushed

TRIM off large leaves of broccoli, and remove tough ends of lower stalks. Wash broccoli thoroughly; cut into spears.
COOK in a small amount of boiling water 10 to 12 minutes, or just until tender. Drain and chill thoroughly.
COMBINE remaining ingredients, stirring well. Pour over chilled broccoli.
YIELD: 4 servings.

Zucchini and Corn Sauté

2 med. zucchini, thinly sliced
1 med. green pepper, thinly
sliced
1 can whole kernel corn,
divided
1 med. sweet red pepper,
thinly sliced
2 to 3 T. vegetable oil (opt.)
1/2 tsp. Italian seasoning

IN a large skillet, sauté zucchini and peppers in oil until crisp-tender, about 4 minutes. Add remaining ingredients; sauté 3 to 4 minutes longer, or until the corn is tender.
YIELD: 10 servings.

Vegetables

SANDWICHES

List Your Favorite Recipes

Recipes   **Page**

_____   _____

_____   _____

_____   _____

_____   _____

_____   _____

_____   _____

_____   _____

_____   _____

_____   _____

_____   _____

_____   _____

_____   _____

_____   _____

_____   _____

_____   _____

Bacon-Cheese Sandwiches

4 slices rye or light wheat
    bread
2 T. mayonnaise
2 ripe avocados, peeled &
    thinly sliced
1 med. onion, thinly sliced

1 (4 oz.) can whole green
    chilies, drained & cut
    in strips
1 or 2 tomatoes, sliced
8 slices bacon, crisply cooked
4 oz. thinly-sliced Cheddar
    cheese

SPREAD bread with mayonnaise.
LAYER each slice with avocado, onion, chilies, tomato and 2 strips bacon. Top with cheese slices.
BROIL for about 5 minutes, or until cheese is melted.
YIELD: 4 servings.

BBQ Ham Sandwiches

1/4 c. chopped onion
1/4 c. butter or margarine
1 c. chili sauce
3/4 c. water

2 T. vinegar
2 T. ground mustard or Dijon
1 lb. thinly-sliced cooked ham
8 English muffins, split

IN a large saucepan, sauté onion in butter; add chili sauce, water, vinegar, brown sugar and mustard. Bring to a boil.
REDUCE heat; cover and simmer for 20 minutes.
ADD ham; return to a boil.
REDUCE heat; cover and simmer for 10 minutes, or until heated through.
SPOON about 1/2 cup to each muffin.
YIELD: 8 servings.

Barbecued Pork Sandwiches

1 pork shoulder roast,
  about 5 lb., trimmed
  & cut into 1" cubes
2 med. onions, coarsely
  chopped
2 T. chili powder

1/2 tsp. salt (opt.)
1 1/2 c. water
1 c. ketchup
1/4 c. vinegar
Hamburger rolls, split

IN a Dutch oven, combine meat, onions, chili powder, and salt if desired, water, ketchup and vinegar.
COVER and simmer for 4 hours, or until the meat falls apart easily. Skim off excess fat.
WITH a slotted spoon, remove meat, reserving cooking liquid.
SHRED the meat with 2 forks or a pastry blender. Return to the cooking liquid and heat through.
YIELD: 16 servings.

Barbecued Pork Sandwiches

6 lb. pork shoulder, bone	1/4 c. lemon juice
in, trimmed of fat & skin	1 med. onion, diced
3 cloves garlic, minced	2 T. dark brown sugar
1 1/2 c. tomato juice	6 T. Worcestershire sauce
1 (28 oz.) can plum tomatoes	1/2 tsp. salt
1 bay leaf	1/4 tsp. cayenne pepper
1 /2 c. distilled white vinegar	1/2 tsp. cinnamon

RUB the pork with the minced garlic. Place in large, heavy stockpot, and add the tomato juice, the tomatoes and their liquid, the bay leaf and 1/4 cup of the vinegar.

BRING to a boil over medium-high heat.

REDUCE the heat to medium-low and break up the tomatoes with a wooden spoon.

COVER and cook, turning the meat occasionally, until it is very tender and beginning to fall apart. (This will usually take about 3 hours.)

ADD the remaining vinegar and all other ingredients to the pork.

COOK, uncovered, over medium-low heat until the pork shreds easily (about another 3 hours).

BE sure to stir about every 1/2 hour.

REMOVE the pork and discard the bones, return to pan and stir another 30 minutes, stirring frequently to break up any larger pieces of meat.

REFRIGERATE for several hours, remove excess fat, reheat and serve.

(I usually add some extra barbecue sauce; use your favorite brand.)

YIELD: 10 to 12 servings.

Calzones

1 1/2 (32 oz.) pkg. frozen
    bread dough
1 lb. ground pork sausage,
    cooked & drained
1/2 lb. ground baked ham
1/2 lb. ground salami
1 c. shredded Swiss cheese
3 T. butter or margarine,
    melted

1 c. shredded Mozzarella
    cheese
1 c. shredded Provolone cheese
2 c. shredded mild Cheddar
    cheese
1/4 c. chopped ripe olives
1 c. chopped onion
3 jalapeño peppers, seeded
    & chopped

ALLOW frozen bread dough to rise according to package directions.
COMBINE sausage and next 9 ingredients, stirring well.
ROLL 1 loaf of dough into a 9x11-inch rectangle on a lightly-floured surface.
PLACE 3 1/2 cups sausage mixture on 1 short side of dough; fold dough over sausage mixture, and pinch edges to seal. Place on a lightly-greased baking sheet and brush with 1 tablespoon butter. Repeat with remaining dough, sausage mixture and butter.
BAKE at 300° for 30 minutes, or until golden. Let stand 5 minutes; slice each into 3 or 4 portions with an electric knife, and serve warm.
YIELD: 9 to 12 servings.

Sandwiches

Creamed Ham and Chicken Sandwiches

1/2 c. sliced fresh mushrooms	1/2 tsp. white pepper
1/4 c. diced green onions	1/4 tsp. dried rosemary
1/4 c. diced red pepper	1 c. diced, cooked chicken
1 T. margarine	breast
3 T. cornstarch	1 c. diced, cooked lean ham
1 c. 2% milk, divided	1/2 c. grated Swiss cheese
1/4 c. dry white wine	3 English muffins, split &
1/2 c. chicken broth	toasted
1/2 tsp. thyme	Parsley, for garnish

SAUTÉ mushrooms, green onion and bell pepper in margarine until vegetables are just tender.

COMBINE cornstarch with 1/4 cup milk, blending well.

ADD cornstarch liquid, 3/4 cup milk, wine, broth, thyme, white pepper and rosemary to vegetables. Simmer, stirring constantly, until thickened. Add chicken, ham and cheese to sauce.

HEAT, stirring constantly, until cheese is melted.

SPREAD chicken and ham mixture on toasted muffin halves.

GARNISH with parsley.

YIELD: 6 servings.

Golden Sausage Boats

12 pork sausage links	Dash of salt
6 eggs	6 frankfurter buns
1/3 c. milk	

PLACE links in an unheated skillet. Do not prick skins.

COOK, covered, 5 minutes over low heat. Uncover, drain off liquid. Finish cooking links over low heat, turning until well browned on all sides.

MEANWHILE, beat together eggs, milk and salt. Dip buns in mixture.

GRILL on both sides until browned.

PLACE sausages in buns.

SERVE with syrup.

YIELD: 6 servings.

Sandwiches

Greek Pita Sandwiches

1 (8 oz.) ctn. sour cream	1 c. diced, peeled cucumbers
1 tsp. dill weed	1/4 tsp. seasoned salt
1/4 c. olive or vegetable oil	1/4 c. lemon juice
2 T. Dijon mustard	2 garlic cloves, minced
1 1/2 tsp. dried oregano	1 tsp. dried thyme
1 1/4 lb. lean boneless pork,	6 pita breads, halved
thinly sliced	1 med. tomato, chopped
2 T. chopped onion	

IN a small bowl, combine sour cream, cucumber, dill and seasoned salt; cover and chill for 6 hours or overnight.

IN a large, resealable plastic bag, combine oil, lemon juice, mustard, garlic, oregano and thyme; add pork. Seal bag and turn to coat; chill for 6 hours or overnight, turning occasionally.

DRAIN and discard marinade. In a skillet over medium heat, stir-fry pork for about 4 minutes, or until no longer pink.

STUFF into pita breads; top with cucumber sauce, tomato and onion.

GARNISH with parsley sprigs and fresh fruit.

YIELD: 6 servings.

Grilled Ham and Cheese Sandwich

3 c. shredded cabbage	2/3 c. mayonnaise
1/3 c. chutney	1 T. curry powder
1/8 tsp. salt	12 (1 oz.) slices cooked ham
6 slices Cheddar cheese	12 slices rye bread
1/4 c. butter, softened	

COMBINE first 5 ingredients; set aside.

PLACE 2 ham slices, 1/2 cup slaw, and 1 cheese slice onto 6 bread slices; top with remaining slices of bread.

SPREAD half of butter on outside of one side of each sandwich. Place, buttered-side down, on hot griddle or skillet. Cook 1 minute, or until golden.

SPREAD remaining butter on ungrilled side, and cook until golden and cheese begins to melt. Serve immediately.

YIELD: 6 servings.

THIS sandwich would taste great with gazpacho soup in the summer, or tomato soup in the winter months, and chocolate brownies for dessert.

Ham Burgers

3/4 lb. ground smoked ham	1/3 c. milk
1/2 lb. ground beef	2 T. brown sugar
1 beaten egg	1 1/2 tsp. dry mustard
1/2 c. bread crumbs	

COMBINE all ingredients and shape into 6 patties.
BROIL or grill for 10 minutes on each side.

Ham and Cheese in the Round

1 lb. round sourdough bread, or 6 hoagie buns	2 med.-size red or green peppers, cut into thin strips
1/2 c. mayonnaise or salad dressing	1 stalk celery, sliced
2 1/2 tsp. dried Italian seasoning	1 T. olive oil
1/2 tsp. pepper	1 lb. cooked ham, thinly sliced
1 lg. onion, thinly sliced	1 1/2 c. (6 oz.) shredded Cheddar & Mozzarella cheese blend

SLICE off top third of bread loaf; set top aside. Hollow out bottom section, leaving a 1/2-inch shell.

COMBINE mayonnaise, Italian seasoning and pepper. Brush inside of bread shell with half of mixture. Set shell and remaining mixture aside.

COOK onion, pepper strips and celery in oil in a large skillet over medium-high heat until tender, stirring often.

ARRANGE half of ham in bread shell and top with half of vegetable mixture; sprinkle with half of cheese.

SPREAD remaining mayonnaise mixture over cheese. Repeat layers with remaining ham, vegetable mixture and cheese. Replace bread top.

WRAP sandwich in heavy-duty aluminum foil.

BAKE at 400° for 30 minutes, or until thoroughly heated. Cut into wedges; serve immediately.

YIELD: 6 servings.

Ham and Pineapple Pizza

1 (12") refrigerated baked
    pizza crust
2 tsp. olive oil
1 c. pizza sauce
2 c. chopped smoked ham

1 (20 oz.) can pineapple
    tidbits, well drained
1/2 c. (2 oz.) shredded
    Mozzarella cheese
1 c. (4 oz.) Provolone cheese

BRUSH pizza crust with olive oil, and spread pizza sauce evenly over crust. Top sauce evenly with ham and pineapple; sprinkle with cheese. BAKE at 425° for 10 minutes, or until cheese melts and crust is lightly browned.
YIELD: 1 (12-inch) pizza.

Sandwiches

Ham and Spinach Pizza

1/4 lb. thinly-sliced country ham	1 (10 oz.) pkg. frozen, chopped spinach, cooked & drained
2/3 c. Roasted Garlic Sauce (see below)	1 c. (4 oz.) shredded Mozzarella cheese
1 (12") refrigerated pizza crust	1/2 c. grated Parmesan cheese

COOK ham according to package directions and cut into thin strips.
SPREAD Roasted Garlic Sauce over pizza crust; top with ham, spinach and cheese.
BAKE at 425° for 10 minutes, or until bubbly.
YIELD: 1 (12-inch) pizza.

ROASTED GARLIC SAUCE:	1 1/2 T. butter or margarine
2 heads garlic, unpeeled	1 1/2 T. all-purpose flour
1 tsp. olive oil	2/3 c. chicken broth

PLACE garlic on a piece of aluminum foil and drizzle with olive oil. Fold edges together to seal.
BAKE at 425° for 30 minutes; cool.
MELT butter in a heavy saucepan over medium-high heat. Cut top off each garlic bread and squeeze cooked garlic into pan (it will be soft and sticky).
ADD flour, and cook, stirring constantly with a wire whisk, 1 minute or until lightly browned.
ADD chicken broth. Cook, stirring constantly, until mixture is thick and bubbly.
YIELD: 2/3 cup.

Ham Reubens

8 oz. fully-cooked ham, julienned	8 oz. Swiss cheese, julienned
3/4 c. mayonnaise	1 (8 oz.) can sauerkraut, drained
1 tsp. caraway seed	Dijon mustard (opt.)
8 slices rye bread	

COMBINE ham, cheese, mayonnaise, sauerkraut and caraway.
LIGHTLY toast the bread. Spread mustard on toast if desired; top with filling.
PLACE on a baking sheet; broil 6 inches from heat for 2 to 3 minutes, or until cheese melts.
YIELD: 4 to 8 servings.

Ground Pork Loaf for Sandwiches

3 T. crushed corn flakes	1 egg
3 T. onions, chopped	1 tsp. sugar
3/4 c. bread crumbs	Salt & pepper
1 T. dried parsley	1 to 2 lb. ground pork

BAKE in ring mold; place crushed corn flakes on the bottom of pan.
MIX the remaining ingredients and place on top of corn flakes.
BAKE at 350° for 30 minutes; drain.
BAKE 30 additional minutes.
TO SERVE, allow to cool for 10 minutes; slice, and make sandwiches using your choice of bread and garnishes.
YIELD: 8 to 10 servings.

Sandwiches

Homemade Sausage and Mushroom Pizza

This pizza was always a favorite Sunday night supper.

PIZZA DOUGH:

2 c. warm water	5 c. flour
2 pkg. active dry yeast	2 tsp. salt

COMBINE the yeast in the warm water. Add mixture to flour and salt with a wooden spoon until moistened.
TURN onto a floured board and knead for 5 to 7 minutes.
PLACE in oiled bowl, turning until all sides are oiled; allow to rise (about 2 hours).
PUNCH down, turn out on floured board, cover with bowl and allow to rest 15 minutes.
ROLL on floured board and place on a baking sheet that has been dusted with cornmeal.

SAUCE:

2 T. vegetable oil	1/2 tsp. salt
2 cloves garlic, minced	2 tsp. oregano
1 sm. can tomato paste	1 tsp. crushed red pepper (opt.)
2 sm. cans tomato sauce	2 T. sugar
1/2 c. water	2 med. onions, chopped

MIX all ingredients; bring to a boil.
SIMMER for 25 minutes, stirring occasionally.
REMOVE from heat and set aside.

TOPPING:

1 lb. hamburger	1/2 tsp. salt
1 lb. sausage	2 tsp. oregano
2 sm. onions, chopped	2 sm. cans mushrooms, drained

BROWN meats, onions and spices, mixing well.
DRAIN well, and set aside.

TO assemble pizza: 16 ounces Mozzarella cheese, or more if desired.
COVER dough with sauce, spread well to desired thickness.
ADD Mozzarella cheese to cover.
ADD meat and mushroom topping.
BAKE at 425° for 20 to 25 minutes.

Sandwiches

107

Hot Ham Sandwiches

1/4 c. butter or margarine, softened	2 tsp. poppy seeds or sesame seeds
2 T. finely-chopped onion	6 hamburger buns
2 T. mustard with horseradish	6 slices cooked ham
	6 slices Swiss cheese

COMBINE butter, onion, mustard and poppy seeds; stir well. Spread on both sides of hamburger buns.

PLACE 1 cooked ham slice and 1 Swiss cheese slice on bottom of each sandwich in aluminum foil, and bake at 350° for 25 minutes.
YIELD: 6 servings.

Italian Sausage Broiled Sandwiches

1/2 lb. bulk Italian sausage	1 1/2 c. (6 oz.) shredded Mozzarella cheese
1/2 tsp. dried basil	4 English muffins, split, toasted & buttered
1/2 tsp. dried oregano	
1 (8 oz.) can tomato sauce with mushrooms (may use plain)	

BROWN sausage in skillet, stirring to crumble. Drain excess fat.

ADD basil, oregano and tomato sauce. Simmer until thoroughly heated.

SPRINKLE 1 tablespoon cheese on each half of muffin. Spoon on sausage mixture and sprinkle with remaining cheese.

BROIL 3 inches from heat until cheese is melted.
YIELD: 8 servings.

Layered Ham and Cheese Sandwich

2 slices cooked ham	1/8 c. ripe olives
(about 2 oz.)	1 slice Provolone cheese
3 slices Genoa salami	1 slice Swiss cheese
2 slices pastrami	1 (5") sandwich bun with
1/8 c. green olives	sesame seeds
1/4 c. mayonnaise	1/4 c. Dijon mustard

MIX mayonnaise and Dijon mustard together well.
SPREAD a thin layer of mayonnaise and mustard on top and bottom of bun.
LAYER remaining ingredients on bottom bun; top with top bun and
wrap in aluminum foil.
BAKE at 350° for 20 minutes, or until thoroughly heated.
YIELD: 1 serving.

YOU may increase this recipe for however many servings you wish.

Meat Loaf

Good main dish or good sandwich makings.

1 lb. ground chuck	1/2 c. minced parsley (1/4 c. dry)
1 lb. ground pork	2 lg. eggs
2 T. prepared horseradish (opt.)	1/4 c. milk
1 tsp. salt, or to taste	2 c. fresh bread crumbs
1 tsp. dry mustard	1/4 c. ketchup
1 tsp. dried thyme	3 slices bacon
2 med. onions, chopped	

PLACE onions, meat, horseradish, salt, mustard and herbs in a large
bowl and mix well.
ADD slightly-beaten eggs and milk together; add to meat mixture and
mix well. Sprinkle bread crumbs over mixture and thoroughly mix all
ingredients together.
PLACE in a 10x13-inch baking dish or jellyroll pan, shaping into a
loaf. Top with ketchup, and lay bacon slices across loaf.
BAKE in preheated 350° oven for about 50 minutes.
REMOVE from oven and let rest 5 minutes in pan. May cover with foil
and wait an additional 5 to 10 minutes before slicing.

Mexican BLT Tortillas

1/2 c. mayonnaise
2 T. ranch salad dressing
8 flour tortillas (7"), warmed
2 to 3 c. shredded lettuce
Green & sweet red pepper
strips (opt.)

1/2 c. sour cream
1/4 tsp. crushed red pepper
flakes
16 bacon strips, cooked
2 c. chopped tomato

IN a bowl, combine mayonnaise, sour cream, salad dressing and red pepper flakes; mix and spread on tortillas.
LAYER with bacon, lettuce and tomato. Top with peppers, if desired.
ROLL up tortillas.
YIELD: 8 servings.

SERVE with warmed refried beans, topped with shredded Cheddar cheese, chopped green onions.
GARNISH with tomato slices and fresh cilantro or parsley.

Mexican Ham Pizza

1 c. sliced fresh mushrooms
1/2 c. chopped green bell
pepper
1 T. vegetable oil
1 c. chopped cooked ham
1 (2 1/4 oz.) can sliced ripe
olives, drained

1 (16 oz.) jar thick & chunky
salsa, divided
1 (8 oz.) pkg. shredded
Monterey Jack & Cheddar
cheese blend
Shredded lettuce
Sour cream

COOK mushrooms and bell pepper in oil in a skillet over medium heat, stirring constantly, until crisp-tender; stir in ham and olives.
Spoon over pizza crust.
RESERVE 1/2 cup salsa; spoon remaining salsa over vegetable mixture.
BAKE at 425° for 10 to 15 minutes. Sprinkle with cheese; bake 5 additional minutes.
SERVE with reserved 1/2 cup salsa, lettuce and sour cream.
YIELD: 1 (12-inch) pizza.

IF you wish a crispier crust, use lower oven rack.

Sandwiches

Peppers and Ham Sandwich

1 red bell pepper
1 green bell pepper
2 hot chili peppers (opt.)
3 green onions
1 T. butter or margarine
1 1/2 c. shredded sharp
  Cheddar cheese
1 (10 oz.) can refrigerated
  pizza dough
1 1/4 lb. thinly-sliced cooked
  ham
1/3 c. thousand island salad
  dressing

CUT peppers into thin strips; slice green onions.
MELT butter in a 10-inch cast-iron skillet over medium-high heat; add peppers and green onions.
COOK, stirring constantly, until tender. Remove from skillet; wipe drippings from skillet and set skillet aside to cool.
UNROLL pizza dough, stretching to a 14 1/2-inch square. Gently place dough in cooled skillet, allowing edges to overhang.
PLACE ham, pepper mixture, salad dressing and cheese on dough; bring corners together in center, forming a knot, and pinch seams to seal.
BAKE at 425° for 15 to 20 minutes, or until golden. Let stand 5 minutes before cutting into wedges.
YIELD: 6 servings.

Pork Burgers

2 lb. lean ground pork
  shoulder
1/4 c. barbecue sauce of choice
Salt, to taste
1/8 tsp. Accent seasoning

COMBINE all ingredients together; mix well.
GRILL or broil 10 minutes on each side.

Pork Burgers

1 lb. lean ground pork	1 sm. jalapeño pepper, seeds
1 T. minced fresh ginger	& membranes removed
2 green onions, trimmed &	(if desired) & cut in thin
cut into thin rounds	rounds
4 hamburger buns, or 1 loaf	2 tsp. soy sauce
Italian bread	

PLACE pork, ginger, onions, pepper and soy sauce in a medium-size bowl. Mix until thoroughly combined. Form into 4 patties.

GRILL on medium-hot coals 6 minutes on each side, or until juices run clear (you may pan-fry these burgers if you wish).

SERVE either on buns or Italian bread, with mayonnaise, lettuce and tomatoes; or use your imagination.

Pork Submarine Sandwich

2 (1 lb.) loaves French	8 slices pickle & pimento beef
bread	8 slices summer sausage
1 (3 oz.) pkg. cream cheese,	4 c. torn romaine or iceberg
softened	lettuce
2 T. chopped chives, or 1 T.	1 med. tomato, chopped &
dry	drained
8 slices cooked ham	2 T. commercial Italian
8 slices salami	salad dressing
1/3 c. pimento-stuffed olives,	
sliced	

CUT bread loaves into quarters crosswise; split each quarter horizontally. Set bread aside.

COMBINE cream cheese, mayonnaise and chives; stir well. Spread about 1 tablespoon mayonnaise mixture on inside cut surface of each piece of bread.

FOLD the meat slices in half; arrange 1 folded slice of each type of meat on bread bottoms; set aside.

COMBINE lettuce, tomato, olives and Italian dressing; toss gently.

SPOON salad mixture over meat slices; cover with bread tops. Serve immediately.

YIELD: 8 servings.

Sausage Burgers

6 (6") French sandwich
    rolls
1 1/2 lb. mild Italian sausage
1 tsp. oregano
4 red or green bell peppers,
    cut into thin strips
1/8 tsp. pepper

1/4 c. chopped onion
1 lg. egg, lightly beaten
1 med. onion, thinly sliced
2 T. vegetable oil
1/2 tsp. salt
1 T. white vinegar

CUT a 3/4-inch slice from the top of each roll; set aside.

SCOOP out bottoms of rolls, leaving 1/2-inch shells; tear bread pieces to measure 1/2 cup fresh bread crumbs. Set shells and bread crumbs aside.

REMOVE and discard casing from sausage; crumble sausage into a large bowl. Add reserved bread crumbs, chopped onion, egg and oregano; knead with your hands to mix well. Divide mixture into 6 equal portions, and shape into 2x5-inch oval patties.

GRILL, covered, over medium-hot coals (350° to 400°), 7 minutes on each side, or until done. Remove from grill and keep warm.

COOK bell pepper strips and onion in oil in a skillet over medium-high heat, stirring constantly, 5 minutes or until crisp-tender. Stir in salt, pepper and vinegar; spoon evenly into bread shells. Top with sausage patties and bread tops; serve immediately.

YIELD: 6 servings.

Two-Pizza Cheese and Sausage Sandwich

1/2 lb. Italian sausage
1/4 c. chopped onion
1/4 c. chopped green pepper
1 (4 1/2 oz.) can sliced
   mushrooms, drained
2 T. sliced pimento-stuffed
   olives

1/2 tsp. dried whole oregano
1 c. (4 oz.) shredded
   Mozzarella cheese, divided
2 (10.1 oz.) frozen cheese
   pizzas
Extra pimento-stuffed olives

REMOVE casings from sausage, and crumble sausage into a large skillet; add onion, green pepper, sliced mushrooms, 2 tablespoons sliced olives and oregano.

COOK over medium heat until meat is browned; drain well and stir in 1/2 cup cheese.

PLACE one pizza on a lightly-greased baking sheet, cheese-side up.

SPOON sausage mixture over pizza; top with second pizza, cheese-side down.

WRAP sandwich securely in aluminum foil.

BAKE at 375° for 15 minutes.

REMOVE foil and bake an additional 10 minutes.

SPRINKLE remaining Mozzarella cheese on top of sandwich; bake an additional 5 minutes.

GARNISH sandwich with sliced olives.

CUT into wedges to serve.

YIELD: 4 to 6 servings.

Turkey-Ham-Prime Sandwich

3/4 lb. sliced pork rib roast
3/4 lb. cooked turkey, sliced
3/4 lb. ham, sliced
3/4 lb. Swiss cheese, thinly
    sliced
12 slices cheese bread, or
    bread of choice

1 head green leaf lettuce
3 med. tomatoes, sliced
Thousand island dressing,
    to taste
Marinated vegetables (recipe
    to follow)

FOR each sandwich, assemble in following order; on one slice of bread, spread thousand island dressing. Place 2 slices rib roast, 2 slices turkey, 3 slices ham and 1 or 2 slices cheese.

FOLD meats individually and top sandwich with an additional slice of bread spread with thousand island dressing.

SECURE sandwich with long toothpicks and cut in half at an angle.

SERVE with a leaf of lettuce and sliced tomatoes on side. You may also accompany your sandwich with marinated vegetables, if desired.

Zesty Italian Loaf

3 T. mayonnaise
1 tsp. prepared mustard
1 garlic clove, minced
1 unsliced loaf Italian
    bread (1 lb.)
6 thin slices tomato
6 thin slices red onion

2 T. butter or margarine,
    softened
1/8 tsp. crushed red pepper
    flakes
6 slices Mozzarella cheese
6 thin slices salami
12 thin slices pepperoni

IN small bowl, combine the first 5 ingredients; set aside.

MAKE 11 slices in the bread, not cutting all the way through bottom crust.

PLACE loaf on a piece of foil large enough to wrap it completely.

GENTLY separate every other slice and spread 1 tablespoon mayonnaise mixture on cut surfaces.

INSERT cheese, tomato, salami, onion and pepperoni between every other slice.

WRAP foil tightly around loaf; place on a baking sheet.

BAKE at 350° for 25 minutes.

TO SERVE, cut bread between unstuffed slices; serve warm.

YIELD: 6 servings.

Sandwiches   115

Notes &
Recipes

_____
_____
_____
_____
_____
_____
_____
_____
_____
_____
_____
_____
_____
_____
_____
_____
_____
_____
_____

Sandwiches

CASSEROLES

List Your Favorite Recipes

Recipes   **Page**

_____   _____

_____   _____

_____   _____

_____   _____

_____   _____

_____   _____

_____   _____

_____   _____

_____   _____

_____   _____

_____   _____

_____   _____

_____   _____

_____   _____

_____   _____

_____   _____

Bacon Quiche

1 (9") pie crust	1 T. Dijon mustard
2 tsp. olive oil	1/8 tsp. black pepper
1/2 c. mushrooms, sliced	1 c. medium-sharp Cheddar
2 T. onion, chopped	cheese, shredded
3/4 c. half & half	5 slices bacon, fried &
6 lg. eggs	crumbled

PRICK crust with fork.

BAKE crust in a 350° preheated oven for 15 to 20 minutes, or until lightly browned.

ALLOW to cool.

HEAT olive oil in frying pan; cook mushrooms and onions until soft, about 5 minutes. Set aside.

WHISK eggs with cream, mustard and pepper. Stir in mushrooms, onion and cheese; pour into crust.

BAKE 35 to 40 minutes, or until set.

LET cool 10 minutes.

Cast-Iron Skillet Pie

1 lb. thinly-sliced ham, cut into strips	1/4 c. sweet banana peppers, seeded & cut in half lengthwise
1/2 c. thousand island dressing	2 green onions, sliced
3 T. butter or margarine, divided	3 c. biscuit & baking mix
1 lg. red pepper, chopped	1 c. milk
	1 (6 oz.) pkg. Provolone cheese slices

TOSS together ham and dressing; set aside.

MELT 2 tablespoons butter in a 10-inch cast-iron skillet. Add peppers and green onions; sauté until tender. Remove vegetables from skillet; set aside. Clean skillet with paper towels.

MELT remaining butter in skillet; set aside.

STIR together baking mix and milk. Turn onto a lightly-floured surface. Shape into a ball; knead 3 to 4 times. Roll dough into a 14 1/2-inch circle. Gently fit into skillet, allowing edges to overhang.

LAYER with ham mixture, vegetable mixture and cheese. Fold sides of dough over edge of cheese and loosely crimp with fingers (as a pie dough).

BAKE at 425° for 15 to 18 minutes, or until golden brown. Let stand 5 minutes; cut into wedges.

YIELD: 6 servings.

Easy Pork Casserole

2 c. cubed, cooked pork	1 (10 3/4 oz.) can cream of mushroom soup, undiluted
1 tsp. onion powder	1 (10 3/4 oz.) can cream of celery soup
1/2 tsp. garlic powder	
1/2 tsp. dried basil	2 c. cooked green peas
1/2 tsp. dried thyme	1 sm. can water chestnuts, diced & drained
Salt & pepper, to taste	
1 can French-fried onions	

COMBINE all ingredients, other than the can of French-fried onions. Mix well.

PLACE mixture in a greased 9x13x2-inch baking dish.

TOP with can of French-fried onions.

BAKE at 350° for 30 to 40 minutes, or until bubbly.

SERVE while hot, with garlic bread or bread of your choice.

Ham á la King

2 T. butter or margarine	3/4 tsp. dry mustard
1/2 c. diced green pepper	1/2 tsp. salt
3 T. sliced green onions	3 hard-cooked eggs, coarsely
1 c. fresh mushrooms	chopped
1 (10 oz.) pkg. frozen peas,	1 (10 oz.) pkg. frozen puff
cooked & drained	pastry shells, baked
2 c. cubed fully-cooked ham	

IN skillet, melt butter over medium heat; add green pepper, onions and mushrooms. Cook and stir until tender.
STIR in peas, ham, mustard and salt; heat through. Gently stir in eggs; set aside.

WHITE SAUCE:	1/4 tsp. salt
1/4 c. butter or margarine	Dash of white pepper
1/4 c. all-purpose flour	2 c. milk

MELT butter in a saucepan; add flour, salt and pepper. Stir to make a smooth paste.
ADD milk all at once; cook and stir until thickened and bubbly, then cook 1 minute more.
ADD ham mixture and heat through.
SERVE in pastry shells.
YIELD: 6 servings.

THIS would taste great with fresh grapes, oranges, etc., during the summer, or with a dish of warmed, chunky cinnamon applesauce in the winter.

Ham and Cornbread Squares

1 (10 oz.) can diced
    tomatoes with green
    chilies, undrained
1/4 c. chopped onion
1 garlic clove, minced
1/2 c. cornmeal
2 eggs
3/4 c. milk
3 T. vegetable oil
Salsa (opt.)

1 T. cornstarch
1 lb. diced, fully-cooked ham
2 tsp. chili powder
1 c. all-purpose flour
2 tsp. baking powder
1 (16 oz.) can whole kernel
    corn, drained
1 1/2 c. (6 oz.) shredded
    Monterey Jack cheese

DRAIN tomatoes, reserving juice in a skillet; set tomatoes aside.
ADD cornstarch to juice; mix well. Add ham, onion, chili powder, garlic and tomatoes. Bring to a boil over medium heat. Boil and stir 2 minutes. Set aside.
IN a bowl, combine flour, cornmeal and baking powder.
IN another bowl, combine eggs, corn, milk and oil. Stir into dry ingredients just until moistened.
SPREAD half the batter into a greased 9-inch square baking dish.
SPOON meat mixture over batter. Sprinkle with cheese.
SPOON remaining batter on top.
BAKE, uncovered, at 350° for 35 to 40 minutes, or until golden brown.
LET stand before cutting.
SERVE with salsa, if desired.
YIELD: 6 servings.
SERVE with fresh fruit.

Casseroles

Ham and Hash Brown Potato Casserole

1 (26 oz.) pkg. frozen hash brown potatoes	1/2 tsp. pepper
	1/4 c. grated Parmesan cheese
1 (1 lb.) ham slice, cut into bite-size pieces	1 c. (4 oz.) shredded Cheddar cheese
1 (10 3/4 oz.) can undiluted cream of potato soup	Paprika

COMBINE first 4 ingredients in a large bowl; spoon into a lightly-greased 9x13x2-inch baking dish.

BAKE at 400° for 25 minutes; sprinkle with cheeses and paprika. Bake an additional 5 minutes, or until heated through.

YIELD: 4 to 5 servings.

Ham Dijon and Scalloped Potatoes

1 3/4 lb. russet potatoes, peeled	3 T. all-purpose flour
	2 1/2 c. milk
3/4 lb. smoked ham, cut into bite-size pieces	1 T. Dijon mustard
	1/4 tsp. salt
3 T. butter	1/8 tsp. ground pepper

HALVE potatoes lengthwise, then cut crosswise into 1/4-inch-thick slices. Place in a 2-quart casserole and add the ham.

IN a medium-size saucepan, melt butter over medium heat. Add the flour, whisking constantly, until mixture is thickened and bubbly. Slowly add the milk, whisking constantly, and cook, whisking often, until the sauce thickens and comes to a boil.

REDUCE heat to low; add the mustard, salt and pepper. Cook 2 to 3 minutes.

POUR the sauce over the potatoes and ham; stir to coat.

BAKE, uncovered, at 350° for 1 1/2 hours, or until the potatoes are tender.

LET stand, uncovered, for 15 minutes before serving.

YIELD: 8 servings.

Ham Hash

1 lb. fully-cooked ham,
finely ground
3 med. potatoes, peeled &
cooked
2 T. Parmesan cheese,
grated
1 T. prepared mustard
1 tsp. prepared horseradish

1 c. (4 oz.) shredded Cheddar
cheese
1 lg. onion, finely chopped
2 T. butter or margarine, melted
2 tsp. Worcestershire sauce
1/4 tsp. pepper
1/2 c. shredded Monterey Jack
cheese

IN a bowl, combine ham and onion. Shred potatoes and add to ham mixture.

STIR in butter, Parmesan cheese, mustard, Worcestershire sauce, horseradish and pepper.

SPOON into a greased 7x11x2-inch baking dish, pressing down firmly.

COMBINE Cheddar and Monterey Jack cheeses; sprinkle over top.

BAKE, uncovered, at 350° for 35 minutes.

YIELD: 6 servings.

Hot Sesame Pork on Mixed Greens

1/2 (16 oz.) pkg. wonton
 wrappers
2 lb. boneless pork loin,
 trimmed
3/4 c. sesame seeds, divided
1 c. vegetable oil, divided
1/2 c. all-purpose flour
1 tsp. salt
1/2 tsp. pepper

1/4 c. dark sesame oil, divided
1/3 c. soy sauce
1/4 c. rice wine vinegar
10 to 12 sm. green onions,
 sliced
1 (10 oz.) pkg. mixed salad
 greens
1 bok choy, shredded

CUT wonton wrappers into 1/2-inch strips; cut pork into 3x1-inch strips. Set aside.

TOAST 1/2 cup sesame seeds in a large, heavy skillet over medium-high heat, stirring constantly, 2 to 3 minutes. Remove from skillet.

POUR 1/2 cup vegetable oil into skillet; heat to 375°. Fry wonton strips in batches until golden. Drain on paper towels; set aside. Drain skillet.

COMBINE remaining 1/4 cup sesame seeds, flour, salt and pepper in a heavy-duty zip-top plastic bag; add pork. Seal and shake to coat.

POUR 2 tablespoons sesame oil into skillet; place over medium heat. Fry half of pork in hot oil, stirring often, 6 to 8 minutes, or until golden. Remove and keep warm. Repeat procedure with remaining 2 table-spoons sesame oil and pork.

PROCESS toasted sesame seeds, remaining 1/2 cup vegetable oil, soy sauce and vinegar in a blender, 1 to 2 minutes, or until smooth.

COMBINE pork and green onions; drizzle with soy sauce mixture, tossing gently.

COMBINE mixed greens and bok choy with pork mixture and fried wonton strips.

SERVE immediately.

YIELD: 8 servings.

Casseroles   123

Italian Pork Supper

4 boneless pork chops	1/8 tsp. black pepper
1 T. vegetable oil	1/2 tsp. garlic salt
1/4 lb. Italian bulk sausage	1/2 tsp. dried oregano, crushed
1/2 c. chopped onion	1 tsp. cornstarch
1 (8 oz.) can tomato sauce	2 T. cold water
3/4 c. apple juice or cider	

SAUTÉ chops in oil in skillet, turning to brown on both sides. Remove chops from pan; set aside.

SAUTÉ sausage and onion in skillet until sausage is cooked, stirring to crumble. Drain excess grease.

ADD tomato sauce, apple juice, black pepper, garlic salt and oregano to sausage mixture. Bring to a boil. Add chops and simmer, covered, for 10 minutes.

REMOVE chops from skillet; keep warm. Blend cornstarch and water until smooth. Add to sauce and cook, stirring often, until bubbly and thickened.

POUR sauce over chops and serve with your favorite pasta.

YIELD: 4 servings.

Italian Sausage Casserole

1 lb. bulk Italian sausage	3 c. mashed potatoes
1 c. chopped onion	3/4 c. chopped green pepper
2 garlic cloves, minced	1 T. cooking oil
2 c. sliced, fresh mushrooms	2 c. chopped fresh tomatoes
1 (2 1/4 oz.) can sliced ripe	1 tsp. dried basil
olives, drained	1/4 tsp. salt
1/8 tsp. pepper	1/4 c. grated Parmesan cheese
2 tsp. dried parsley flakes	

IN a skillet, cook sausage until no longer pink; drain. Place in a greased 9-inch square baking dish. Top with potatoes.

IN the same skillet, sauté onion, green pepper and garlic in oil for 5 minutes, or until vegetables are crisp-tender. Stir in the mushrooms, tomatoes, olives, basil, salt and pepper.

SPOON over potatoes to within 1-inch of edge of dish. Sprinkle Parmesan cheese and parsley over top.

BAKE, covered, at 350° for 30 to 35 minutes, or until top is lightly browned.

YIELD: 4 to 6 servings.

Mexican Pork Stew

1 lb. boneless pork, trimmed & cut into 3/4" cubes	1 1/2 tsp. ground cumin
	1/4 tsp. salt
1/8 tsp. cayenne pepper	2 tsp. cooking oil
2 med. green peppers, cut into 3/4" cubes	2 sm. onions, quartered
	2 garlic cloves, minced
2 med. potatoes, peeled & cubed	1 (14 1/2 oz.) can Mexican-style stewed tomatoes
1 1/2 c. V8 juice	1/2 c. water
1 (10 oz.) pkg. frozen whole kernel corn	Minced fresh cilantro or parsley (opt.)

IN a large resealable plastic bag, combine pork, cumin, salt and cayenne. Shake to coat evenly.

IN a Dutch oven or soup kettle over medium heat, brown pork in oil. Drain.

ADD green peppers, onions and garlic; sauté for 3 minutes.

ADD potatoes, tomatoes, V8 and water; mix well. Bring to a boil. Reduce heat; cover and simmer for 10 to 15 minutes, or until vegetables and pork are tender.

GARNISH with cilantro or parsley, if desired.

YIELD: 6 to 8 servings.

SERVE with hot, crusty bread and butter, sprinkled with Parmesan cheese.

Pasta and Italian Sausages

1 (8 oz.) pkg. pasta of your
    choice
1 lb. Italian sausage
1 onion, chopped
2 cloves garlic, minced
1 (28 oz.) can whole
    tomatoes, cut up &
    undrained
1 (8 oz.) can tomato sauce

1 (4 oz.) can mushrooms,
    drained
1 1/2 tsp. basil
1 tsp. thyme
1 tsp. salt
1/2 tsp. chili powder
3 T. sugar
1 c. Mozzarella cheese

COOK pasta according to package directions; drain and set aside.
COOK sausage, onion and garlic; drain.
ADD tomatoes, sauce and seasonings.
COOK and simmer 10 minutes.
TO SERVE: Pour sauce over pasta and top with cheese.

THIS dish tastes great with hot garlic bread, Caesar salad, and your
favorite dessert.

Pork and Cabbage Shepherd's Pie

PORK LAYER:

1 lb. ground pork	1 sm. onion, chopped
2 garlic cloves, minced	1 c. cooked rice
1/2 c. pork gravy, or 1/4 c.	1/2 tsp. salt
chicken broth	1/2 tsp. dried thyme

CABBAGE LAYER:	1/4 tsp. pepper
1 med. carrot	1 sm. onion, chopped
2 T. butter or margarine	6 c. chopped cabbage
1 c. chicken broth	1/2 tsp. salt

POTATO LAYER:	
2 c. mashed potatoes	1/4 c. shredded Cheddar cheese

IN a skillet over medium heat, brown pork until no longer pink. Add onion and garlic. Cook until vegetables are tender; drain. Stir in rice, gravy, salt and thyme.

SPOON into a greased 7x11x2-inch baking dish.

IN the same skillet, sauté carrot and onion in butter over medium heat for 5 minutes. Stir in cabbage; cook for 1 minute. Add broth, salt and pepper; cover and cook for 10 minutes. Spoon over pork layer.

SPOON or pipe mashed potatoes on top; sprinkle with cheese.

BAKE, uncovered, at 350° for 45 minutes, or until browned.

YIELD: 6 servings.

Pork and Mushroom Casserole

3/4 lb. pork, cubed into 1/2" pieces	1/2 c. butter or margarine, divided
3 (8 oz.) pkg. sliced fresh mushrooms	1 1/2 c. herb-seasoned stuffing mix
2 c. (8 oz.) shredded sharp Cheddar cheese, divided	1/2 c. half & half

MELT butter in a large skillet over medium-high heat; add sausage and mushrooms; cook, stirring constantly, until tender. Stir in stuffing mix.

SPOON half of mushroom and sausage mixture into an 8-inch square baking dish; sprinkle with half the cheese. Repeat layers; dot with remaining 1/4 cup butter. Pour half over casserole.

BAKE at 325° for 30 minutes.

YIELD: 6 servings.

Pork and Vegetables in a Skillet

4 lean rib pork chops, 1/2" thick	1/4 tsp. sage, crushed
Salt & pepper, to taste	1 (14 to 16 oz.) can whole green beans, drained
2 T. vegetable oil	1 (12 oz.) can whole kernel corn, drained (reserve liquid)
1 onion, sliced	
1 (8 oz.) can tomato sauce	

SEASON the chops with salt and pepper. Brown in vegetable oil in a heavy skillet; remove chops from skillet and set aside.

TO SKILLET, add onion and cook until crisp-tender; stir in tomato sauce and sage.

RETURN chops to skillet; cover and simmer 45 minutes. Add vegetables and reserved liquid (you may have to add even more, if this is not enough).

SIMMER 10 minutes, or until heated through.

YIELD: 4 servings.

Pork Balls on Parslied Noodles

1 lb. ground pork	1 tsp. salt
1 c. soft bread crumbs	1 tsp. lemon juice
1/4 to 1/3 c. milk	1/4 tsp. paprika
1 egg	1/8 tsp. nutmeg
1/4 c. finely-chopped onion	1 T. butter or margarine

SAUCE:

1 T. butter or margarine	1/4 tsp. dry mustard
1 T. flour	1 1/2 c. milk

NOODLES:	2 T. butter or margarine, melted
1 (8 oz.) pkg. egg noodles	2 T. chopped parsley

TO PREPARE PORK BALLS:
COMBINE bread crumbs and milk; allow to soak a few minutes. Add ground pork, egg, onion, salt, lemon juice, paprika and nutmeg; mix well. Shape into 18 to 24 balls.
MELT butter or margarine in a 10-inch skillet.
BROWN pork balls well on all sides, turning as needed. Cover and cook slowly, about 19 minutes, until pork is cooked. Remove pork balls from skillet; keep warm.

PREPARE SAUCE:
ADD butter to skillet; melt. Blend in flour and mustard. Add milk; cook until sauce is thickened, stirring constantly. Return pork balls to skillet; heat thoroughly.

COOK noodles as directed on package. Drain well. Toss with melted butter; sprinkle with parsley.
SERVE pork balls and sauce over noodles.
YIELD: 4 to 6 servings.

Pork Casserole

1/2 lb. lean, boneless pork, trimmed & cut into 3/4" cubes	1/8 tsp. pepper
	1 c. sliced celery
	1/4 c. chopped onion
2 T. water	2 c. cooked noodles
1 (10 3/4 oz.) can condensed cream of chicken soup, undiluted	1 c. frozen peas
	1/4 tsp. salt (opt.)
	3 T. dry bread crumbs

IN a skillet coated with nonstick cooking spray, brown the pork.

ADD celery, onion and water; cover and simmer for 1 hour, or until pork is tender.

REMOVE from the heat; add noodles, soup, peas, salt if desired, and pepper.

TRANSFER to an ungreased 7x11x2-inch baking dish. Sprinkle with crumbs.

BAKE, uncovered, at 350° for 20 minutes, or until bubbly.

Pork Chop Bake

6 (5 oz.) pork chops, trimmed	1/2 tsp. salt (opt.), divided
1 med. onion, thinly sliced	3 med. potatoes, peeled &
into rings	thinly sliced
6 med. carrots, thinly sliced	1 tsp. dried marjoram
3/4 c. milk	3 T. all-purpose flour
1 (10 3/4 oz.) can condensed	
cream of mushroom soup,	
undiluted	

COAT a skillet with nonstick cooking spray; brown pork chops on both sides.

PLACE in an ungreased 9x13x2-inch baking pan; sprinkle with 1/4 teaspoon salt, if desired.

LAYER onion, potatoes and carrots over chips.

SPRINKLE with marjoram, and remaining salt, if desired.

IN a small bowl, stir milk and flour until smooth; add soup. Pour over vegetables.

COVER and bake at 350° for 1 hour. Uncover and bake 15 minutes longer, or until pork and vegetables are tender.

YIELD: 6 servings.

THIS is almost a meal in itself. All you would need is a dessert of your choice.

Pork Chow Mein

1 1/2 lb. lean pork, thinly sliced	1 (8 oz.) can water chestnuts, sliced
1/4 c. cornstarch	1 (1 lb. 4 oz.) can bean sprouts
2 tsp. sugar	1 (4 oz.) can sliced mushrooms, drained
4 T. salad oil	
2 c. water	Salt
1 1/2 c. sliced celery	Pepper
1 c. chopped or sliced onion	1 bunch small green onions
1 T. molasses	Toasted, whole, blanched almonds

CUT meat into thin strips.

COMBINE 2 tablespoons cornstarch and sugar. Blend in 1 tablespoon soy sauce and oil. Let meat stand in this mixture 10 minutes. Brown lightly on all sides in hot oil; add remaining soy sauce and 1 1/2 cups water. Simmer 45 minutes. Add celery and onions; simmer 10 to 15 minutes.

BLEND remaining cornstarch and 1/2 cup water; stir into meat mixture. Add molasses, water chestnuts, bean sprouts and mushrooms. Heat thoroughly. Season with salt and pepper.

GARNISH with green onions and almonds.

YIELD: 8 servings.

Pork Cantonese

2 lb. lean pork, cut in 1"
    pieces
2 T. salad oil
1 (14 oz.) can pineapple
    chunks
1 (4 oz.) can mushrooms
1/3 c. unsulphured molasses

1/4 c. vinegar
2 green peppers, cut into strips
2 onions, sliced & separated
    in rings
1 1/2 T. cornstarch
2 T. water

BROWN pork on all sides in hot oil in skillet.

DRAIN pineapple and mushrooms, reserving liquids. Combine liquids and add enough water to make 2 cups. Add liquid to pork; cover and simmer until tender, about 45 minutes.

STIR in molasses and vinegar until blended. Add pineapple, mushrooms, green peppers and onions; cover and cook 10 minutes.

BLEND together cornstarch and water. Stir into hot mixture and cook until slightly thickened.

SERVE over hot rice.

YIELD: 8 servings.

Pork Roast and Beans

4 lb. pork loin
1/2 tsp. garlic powder
1/2 tsp. salt
1 lb. navy beans

1 c. brown sugar
4 slices bacon
1 c. ketchup

FOR PORK: Season with garlic powder and salt; roast at 350° for 2 1/2 hours.

FOR BEANS: Soak beans overnight; add a pinch of baking soda. Drain water. Add fresh water to cover beans; add a pinch of salt and simmer for 1 1/2 hours, or until tender.

DRAIN beans, leaving a little water in the pot.

CUT bacon into 1/2-inch pieces and fry; once cooked, drain.

ADD bacon drippings, sugar and ketchup to beans; mix well.

ONE-HALF HOUR before pork roast is cooked, spread beans around meat and stir every 10 to 15 minutes, until done.

YIELD: About 8 servings.

NOTE: Be sure to soak your beans overnight before you start to prepare this dish.

Casseroles

Pork Pot Pie

2 T. vegetable oil	1/2 tsp. sage, ground
2/3 c. onion, finely diced	2/3 c. carrot, finely diced
2/3 c. celery, finely diced	1/4 tsp. white pepper
1/4 tsp. garlic, minced	1 c. frozen peas
1 lb. lean pork, ground	1/4 c. chicken stock or broth
1/8 tsp. cloves, ground	Pastry for 2-crust 9" pie

PREHEAT oven to 400°.
HEAT oil in a large skillet over medium heat. Sauté onion until transparent. ADD carrot, celery and garlic; cook 3 to 4 minutes longer. Turn heat to high and add ground pork. Cook and stir until pork is lightly browned. Reduce heat and stir in seasonings, potatoes, peas and chicken stock. Cook 5 minutes, or until potatoes are tender. Remove from heat and cool completely.
WHEN filling is cooled, line a deep-dish 9-inch pie plate with pastry. Add filling and top with remaining pastry.
CUT 2 vent holes in top of crust and bake for 30 to 40 minutes, or until the crust is golden brown.
SERVE hot.
YIELD: 1 (9-inch) pie.

Pork/Sauerkraut Pinwheel

3/4 c. dry bread crumbs	2 lb. ground lean pork
2 eggs, slightly beaten	1 (1 lb.) can sauerkraut, drained
1/3 c. milk	& finely cut with scissors
1 1/2 tsp. salt	1/4 c. chopped onion
1/4 tsp. pepper	1 T. sugar
1 tsp. thyme leaves	3 T. pimento (opt.)
1 T. Worcestershire sauce	5 slices bacon

COMBINE bread crumbs, eggs, milk, salt, pepper, thyme and Worcestershire sauce. Mix in pork.
ON waxed paper, pat pork mixture into a 9x12-inch rectangle.
COMBINE sauerkraut, onion, pimento (if desired), and sugar. Spread evenly over meat. Roll up from narrow end. Place loaf in greased, shallow baking dish; lay bacon over top.
BAKE in a 375° oven for 1 hour and 10 minutes.
YIELD: 8 servings.

Casseroles 135

Pork Stew with Dumplings

This recipe was given to me by a friend from Springfield, IL. My family loved it so much, we have tried variations between pork and beef, and corn dumplings and regular dumplings. I have included a recipe for the regular dumplings.

2 lb. boneless pork, trimmed
   & cut into 3/4" cubes
1 1/4 c. chicken broth,
   divided
2 bay leaves
1 tsp. dried thyme
3/4 tsp. salt
1/4 tsp. garlic powder

2 T. all-purpose flour
2 T. cooking oil
1 (28 oz.) can stewed tomatoes
1 med. onion, quartered
1 tsp. Worcestershire sauce
3/4 tsp. sugar
1/4 tsp. pepper
1/8 tsp. ground nutmeg

IN a large skillet over medium heat, brown pork in oil; drain. Stir in tomatoes, 1 cup broth, onion and seasonings. Bring to a boil.
REDUCE heat; cover and simmer for 60 to 70 minutes, or until pork is tender.
COMBINE flour and remaining broth until smooth; gradually add to stew, stirring constantly. Bring to a boil; boil and stir for 2 minutes. Remove bay leaves.

CORN DUMPLINGS:
1/2 c. all-purpose flour
1 1/2 tsp. baking powder
Dash of pepper
3 T. milk
1 (8 3/4 oz.) can whole
   kernel corn, drained

1/3 c. yellow cornmeal
1/4 tsp. salt
1 egg
2 T. vegetable oil

Continued on following page.

Casseroles

Continued from preceding page.

IN a bowl, combine flour, cornmeal, baking powder, salt and pepper. BEAT egg, milk and oil; add to flour mixture and mix until just moistened. Stir in corn. Drop by rounded tablespoonfuls into simmering stew.
COVER and cook for 10 to 12 minutes, or until dumplings are tender.
YIELD: 6 servings.

PLAIN DUMPLINGS:

1 egg	1/2 tsp. salt
1 T. melted butter	3 tsp. baking powder
6 T. water	1 c. flour

STIR dry mixture into liquid mixture to make a soft dough. Drop into simmering stew by rounded tablespoonfuls. Cook for 12 minutes with lid on pan (do not remove lid during cooking time).

Pork Stroganoff

1 lb. pork loin, cut into strips	1/2 tsp. pepper
4 c. uncooked egg noodles	3 c. sliced mushrooms
4 tsp. vegetable oil	1 pkg. brown gravy mix
1 clove garlic, crushed	1 c. cold water
1/2 tsp. salt	1/2 c. sour cream

COOK egg noodles according to package directions. Keep warm.
IN a large nonstick skillet, heat 2 teaspoons of oil over medium-high heat until hot.
ADD pork and garlic; stir-fry for 1 minute, or until no longer pink. Remove from skillet; season with salt and pepper.
IN same skillet, cook mushrooms in remaining 2 teaspoons of oil for 2 minutes, or until tender, stirring occasionally. Remove skillet from heat. Add brown gravy mix and water; blend well.
RETURN skillet to heat; bring to a boil.
REDUCE heat to low; simmer 1 minute.
RETURN pork to skillet; heat through, about 1 minute.
SERVE over noodles; top with sour cream.
YIELD: 4 servings.

Potatoes and Ham

4 med. potatoes, peeled &
cooked
1/8 tsp. salt
2 to 4 T. milk
3/4 c. diced, fully-cooked
ham
1/4 c. finely-chopped onion

2 T. butter or margarine, melted
1/8 tsp. pepper
1 c. (4 oz.) shredded Cheddar
cheese, divided
1/4 c. finely-chopped green
pepper

IN a large bowl, mash potatoes until smooth. Add butter, salt, pepper, and enough milk to make a soft mashed potato consistency.
STIR in 2/3 cup cheese, ham, onion and green pepper.
TRANSFER to a greased 1 1/2-quart baking dish.
BAKE, uncovered, at 350° for 20 to 25 minutes, or until heated through.
SPRINKLE with remaining cheese.
YIELD: 4 to 6 servings.

Sausage-Vegetable Skillet

1 T. butter or margarine
1 lb. kielbasa sausage, cut
into 1/2" slices
1 head cauliflower, broken
into flowerets
3 carrots, scraped & thinly
sliced

3 zucchini, thinly sliced
1 med. onion, thinly sliced
1/2 tsp. salt
1/4 tsp. pepper
1 c. (4 oz.) shredded Monterey
Jack cheese

MELT butter in a 12-inch skillet over medium-high heat; add sausage and cook until browned, stirring often. Remove with a slotted spoon, reserving drippings in skillet; set sausage aside.
ADD cauliflower and next 3 ingredients to skillet; cook, stirring constantly, 5 minutes, or until crisp-tender. Stir in salt and pepper; cover and reduce heat. Simmer 5 minutes. Stir in sausage; cook just until thoroughly heated.
SPOON mixture into individual baking dishes and sprinkle with cheese. Cover and let stand until cheese melts.
YIELD: 6 servings.

Sausage-Stuffed Shells

1/2 (12 oz.) pkg. jumbo pasta   3/4 c. Italian-seasoned bread
    shells, about 20   crumbs
1 lb. Italian sausage   1 (30 oz.) jar spaghetti sauce
1 lg. egg, lightly beaten   1/4 c. grated Parmesan cheese

COOK jumbo shells according to package directions. Drain and set aside.
REMOVE and discard casings from Italian sausage. Brown sausage in a large skillet, stirring until it crumbles; drain.
COMBINE sausage, egg and bread crumbs in skillet; set aside.
SPREAD 1 cup spaghetti sauce in bottom of a lightly-greased 9x13x2-inch baking dish. Spoon sausage mixture into shells; place in baking dish. Pour remaining sauce over stuffed shells.
BAKE, covered, at 350° for 15 minutes; sprinkle with cheese and bake, uncovered, 5 additional minutes, or until thoroughly heated.
YIELD: 6 servings.

Scalloped Pork Chops

4 pork chops (1/2" thick)   1 T. cooking oil
1/4 c. chopped onion   1 (10 3/4 oz.) can condensed
1/2 c. milk   cream of mushroom soup,
3 c. thinly-sliced, peeled   undiluted
    potatoes   6 c. shredded cabbage
1/4 tsp. salt   1/4 tsp. pepper

IN a skillet over medium heat, brown pork chops in oil; set aside. Reserve 1 teaspoon of drippings; sauté onion in drippings until tender.
BLEND in soup and milk; set aside.
IN a greased 2 1/2-quart casserole, layer half of the potatoes, cabbage, salt and pepper.
POUR 3/4 cup soup mixture on top. Repeat layers of potatoes, cabbage, salt and pepper. Top with pork chops.
COVER and bake at 350° for 50 to 60 minutes, or until pork and vegetables are tender.
YIELD: 4 servings.

SERVE with your choice of Jello topped with whipped topping.

Scalloped Potatoes and Pork Chops

6 pork chops
1 T. vegetable oil
5 c. potatoes, sliced
6 slices American cheese
1 tsp. salt

1/2 c. onions, chopped
1 can cream of mushroom soup
1 1/4 c. milk
1/2 tsp. pepper

BROWN chops in vegetable oil in a heavy skillet; remove chops, reserving pan drippings, and set aside.
PLACE half of the potatoes in a 9x13x2-inch greased baking dish.
TOP with cheese; add the remainder of potatoes and top with pork chops. Add salt and pepper.
COOK onions in reserved pan drippings; add soup and milk. Heat, stirring constantly.
POUR over pork chops.
COVER with foil.
BAKE at 350° for 1 hour.
REMOVE foil and bake an additional 30 minutes.

Sweet and Sour Pork

1 1/2 to 2 lb. cubed pork
1 (29 oz.) can chunk
    pineapple, drained
    (juice reserved)
1/4 c. brown sugar
2 T. cornstarch
1/4 c. vinegar

1 to 2 T. soy sauce
1/2 tsp. salt
1 sm. green pepper, sliced in
    strips
1/4 c. onions, sliced
2 to 3 c. hot, cooked rice

COAT pork in flour and brown in 2 tablespoons of vegetable oil; add 1/2 cup of water. Cover and simmer until tender.
ADD cornstarch, brown sugar, vinegar and soy sauce to the reserved pineapple juice.
STIR until well blended.
ADD mixture to the pork, stirring until gravy thickens.
ADD pineapple, green pepper and onions.
SIMMER 4 to 5 minutes.
SERVE over hot, cooked rice.

Wrapped Asparagus Casserole

10 boiled ham slices
10 spears of asparagus (you
   may use fresh or canned)

1 (10 3/4 oz.) can cream of
   asparagus soup, undiluted
1/2 can milk
3 T. Parmesan cheese

ROLL asparagus spears in ham slices.
ARRANGE in a 7x11-inch lightly-greased baking dish.
MIX soup and milk together; heat through. Pour over asparagus and
ham rolls.
SPRINKLE Parmesan cheese over top.
BAKE at 350° for 20 minutes.

Notes &
Recipes

MAIN DISHES

List Your Favorite Recipes

Recipes   **Page**

_____   _____

_____   _____

_____   _____

_____   _____

_____   _____

_____   _____

_____   _____

_____   _____

_____   _____

_____   _____

_____   _____

_____   _____

_____   _____

_____   _____

_____   _____

_____   _____

_____   _____

_____   _____

Apple Pork Chops

1/4 c. all-purpose flour	1/2 tsp. salt
1/2 tsp. paprika	1/8 tsp. white pepper
6 (1/2" thick) pork chops	1/4 c. vegetable oil
2 med. cooking apples	2 c. apple juice, divided
3 T. brown sugar	1/2 tsp. ground allspice

COMBINE the first 4 ingredients; dredge pork chops in mixture. Brown pork chops in oil in a large skillet. Arrange chops in a 9x13x2-inch baking dish. Core unpeeled apples and cut into rings; place on chops. Pour 1/2 cup apple juice over apples. Combine sugar and allspice; sprinkle over apples.

BAKE, uncovered, at 325° for 1 hour, or until chops are tender.

REMOVE pork chops and apple slices to a serving platter, reserving pan drippings.

DISSOLVE 1 1/2 tablespoons remaining flour mixture in remaining 1/2 cup apple juice.

COMBINE flour mixture and pan drippings in a saucepan; cook over medium heat until thickened, stirring constantly. Serve sauce over pork chops.

YIELD: 6 servings.

Apricot Bourbon Pork
Chef Jeff Corbin

4 (2 oz.) medallions center-
    cut pork loin
1/2 c. teriyaki sauce
2 T. light corn oil
1/2 c. sliced yellow onion

1/2 c. sliced green pepper
1 oz. bourbon
1/4 c. apricot preserves
4 T. Dijon mustard
1 c. cooked wild rice

MARINATE pork 1/2 hour in teriyaki sauce.
HEAT skillet with oil to approximately 300°.
SAUTÉ pork to medium and add vegetables, cooking slightly crisp.
REMOVE from skillet and place over bed of rice.
USING sauté pan, add bourbon to deglaze pan.
ADD preserves and mustard; mix well.
BRING to a light boil.
POUR evenly over pork and vegetables.
SERVE immediately.

NOTE: Do not over-marinate meat, as this will rob of natural flavor and dry it out.

Apple-Stuffed Pork Chops

6 pork loin chops, 1 1/2"
    thick
1/2 c. chopped celery
1/2 c. chopped, unpeeled
    apple
2 T. butter

1/4 tsp. salt
1 1/2 c. raisin bread, cubed
1 orange, sectioned & chopped
1 beaten egg
1/2 tsp. grated orange peel
1/8 tsp. ground cinnamon

CUT a pocket in each pork chop by cutting to center of chop from rib side parallel to rib bone and surface of chop.
COOK celery and apple in butter; toss with remaining ingredients.
SPOON about 1/4 cup stuffing into each slit chop; secure opening with toothpicks.
GRILL over medium coals about 20 minutes.
TURN and grill about 15 to 20 minutes more.
YIELD: 6 servings.

144   ***Main Dishes***

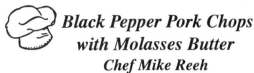

Black Pepper Pork Chops
with Molasses Butter
Chef Mike Reeh

2 lb. boneless pork loin

MOLASSES BUTTER: 1 T. molasses
1/4 c. butter, softened   Juice from 1/2 of fresh lemon

Salt & pepper, to taste

CUT pork loin into 8 pieces (approximately 4 ounces each).
STIR together butter, molasses and lemon juice with a wooden spoon; cover and refrigerate.
RUB chops on both sides evenly with salt and pepper.
GRILL chops over medium-hot coals for 12 to 15 minutes.
TOP each chop with Molasses Butter.
YIELD: 4 servings.

Breaded Pork Chops

2 T. cornmeal	2 T. whole wheat flour
1/2 tsp. rubbed sage	1/2 tsp. sugar
1/2 tsp. paprika	1/4 tsp. onion powder
4 pork chops (1/2" to 3/4" thick)	1/4 c. milk

IN a shallow bowl or large resealable plastic bag, combine the first 7 ingredients.
DIP pork chops into milk, then into the cornmeal mixture. Place on a rack in a shallow baking pan.
BAKE, uncovered, at 425° for 30 to 35 minutes or until juices run clear.
YIELD: 4 servings.

THIS goes well serving with Cheese Potatoes.

Main Dishes

Campfire Pork Dijon
Chef Jeff Corbin

8 oz. pork tenderloin   6 T. apricot preserves
1 oz. vegetable oil   1 T. Dijon mustard

PEEL any silver skin off tenderloin.
CUT tenderloin in 5 (1 1/2-ounce) slices and pound to 1/4-inch thickness.
HEAT oil in skillet and brown each cutlet; check center (pork should be just a little bit pink).
REMOVE pork from pan and set aside; keep warm.
ADD apricot preserves and Dijon mustard to pan; warm and serve over pork.
YIELD: 5 servings.

Cheese-Stuffed Pork Chops

2 scallions   1 tsp. dried thyme
1 (4 oz.) pkg. soft, mild goat   4 (6 oz.) rib pork chops, 1"
   cheese   thick
1 T. white wine   Salt & pepper, to taste
2 T. fresh lemon juice   2 T. vegetable oil
1/2 tsp. ground black pepper   1/2 c. dry white wine

THINLY slice scallions, separating white and green portions.
COMBINE cheese, wine, white portion of scallions, lemon juice, black pepper and thyme, beating until well blended. Chill for 15 minutes or until firm.
CUT a small slit along bone into center of each chop, being careful not to cut through to other side. Spoon cheese mixture into each chop cavity, secure open edge with wooden pick and season with salt and black pepper.
COOK chops in single layer in oil in large skillet over medium heat, covered, for 20 to 25 minutes or until browned and done. Place chops on serving platter and keep warm.
DRAIN excess grease from skillet. Add wine and green part of scallions. Simmer, covered, for 20 to 25 minutes or until sauce is reduced to 1/4 cup. Pour sauce over chops and serve.
YIELD: 4 servings.

Main Dishes

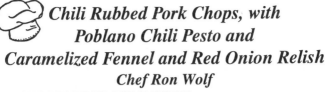

Chili Rubbed Pork Chops, with Poblano Chili Pesto and Caramelized Fennel and Red Onion Relish
Chef Ron Wolf

CHILI RUBBED PORK CHOPS:

1/2 c. chili powder
1 tsp. garlic powder
1 tsp. onion powder
1/4 tsp. ground cumin
1/4 tsp. cayenne pepper

1/2 tsp. salt
1/2 c. olive oil
4 (12 to 14 oz.) center-cut rib
  pork chops, Frenched (have
  butcher cut)

MIX the first 6 ingredients together, and toast in a sauté pan over medium heat, making sure not to burn.

RUB chops with olive oil.

RUB chili powder mixture into both sides of chops and refrigerate for 6 hours.

PREHEAT broiler and boil chops 8 to 10 minutes on each side, or until an internal temperature of 165° is reached.

WHILE chops are broiling, make pesto, and caramelized fennel and red onion relish.

POBLANO CHILI PESTO:

3 T. salted, roasted pepitas
1/2 peeled poblano chili,
  coarsely chopped
2 garlic cloves
1/4 c. firmly-packed cilantro
  leaves

1/4 c. firmly-packed parsley
  leaves
1 T. fresh lime juice
1 T. olive oil
Salt & pepper, to taste
2 T. mayonnaise

Continued on following page.

Continued from preceding page.

IN food processor or blender, with motor running, add the pepitas, peeled chili, and garlic cloves. Process until puréed.

WITH motor still running, add the cilantro, parsley and lime juice; process until puréed.

WITH motor still running, slowly add olive oil in a fine stream, and process until puréed.

ADD salt and pepper to taste.

ADD entire mixture to the 2 tablespoons mayonnaise.

CARAMELIZED FENNEL AND RED ONION RELISH:

1 T. unsalted butter	1 tsp. sugar
1 T. olive oil	12 oz. chicken stock
2 lg. red onions, julienned	Fresh cracked black pepper, to
2 fennel bulbs, trimmed & thinly sliced	taste

IN large sauté pan, heat butter and olive oil over medium heat.

ADD the onions and fennel and cook, stirring often, for 15 minutes or until soft and golden brown.

ADD sugar and continue to cook for another 5 minutes, or until dark brown and caramelized.

POUR in chicken stock and simmer over medium heat until most of the liquid has evaporated.

ADD cracked pepper to taste

TO PLATE ENTRÉE:

PLACE about 1/2 cup of Fennel and Red Onion Relish in center of plate.

PLACE 1 chop off-center of relish and top with 1 1/2 tablespoons of pesto.

GARNISH with cilantro leaves.

Main Dishes

Chinese Roast Pork

4 (8 oz.) pork tenderloins	1/4 c. soy sauce
1/4 c. bourbon	1 clove garlic, minced
1 1/2 T. peeled, minced	1 T. sugar
ginger root	Vegetable cooking spray

TRIM fat from tenderloins; place in a shallow dish.
COMBINE soy sauce and the next 4 ingredients; pour over tenderloins, turning to coat all sides. Cover and chill 2 to 3 hours, turning occasionally.
REMOVE tenderloins from marinade, reserving marinade. Place tenderloins on a rack coated with cooking spray. Place rack in broiler pan; add water to pan. Broil 6 inches from heat for 15 to 18 minutes, turning often, and basting with remaining marinade. Meat is done when meat thermometer inserted in thickest portion of tenderloin registers 160°.
YIELD: 8 servings.

Dijon Pork Chops

1/4 c. red wine vinegar	2 T. Dijon mustard
2 T. vegetable oil	1/4 tsp. dried tarragon
1/2 tsp. fresh chives	4 (4 oz.) butterfly pork chops
2 tsp. chopped fresh parsley	
(1 tsp. dry)	

IN a small bowl, combine the first 6 ingredients; mix well and set aside.
GRILL chops, uncovered, over medium coals for 4 minutes per side (1/2-inch thick) or 6 minutes per side (1-inch thick).
BRUSH with mustard mixture and grill 2 minutes more. Turn, baste and grill 2 more minutes, or until juices run clear.
YIELD: 4 servings.

Main Dishes

Grilled Ham

1 (1" thick) smoked,	3 T. vegetable oil
fully-cooked ham steak	1 T. wine vinegar
(about 2 lb.)	2 tsp. dry mustard
1 c. ginger ale	3/4 tsp. ground ginger
1 c. orange juice	1/2 tsp. ground cloves
1/2 c. firmly-packed brown	
sugar	

SCORE fat edges of ham.

COMBINE remaining ingredients; pour over ham in a shallow baking dish. Refrigerate 8 hours, or let stand at room temperature 1 hour, spooning marinade over ham several times.

GRILL ham over slow coals about 15 minutes on each side, brushing frequently with marinade. Heat remaining marinade and serve with ham.

YIELD: 4 to 6 servings.

Grilled Pork Chops

WHEN you have some meat in your side dishes, you really don't want a very complicated main meat dish.

EASY, quick-grilled pork chops are always good. You may want to rub them with a little vegetable oil, and then a small amount of garlic salt and coarse-ground pepper. Let them sit in refrigerator for about 30 minutes, and grill.

WE always like a fresh fruit salad in the summer, and even some plain canned peaches (or any fruit you prefer) in the winter months. Of course, if you canned or froze last summer, you will always have your own fresh fruit at your fingertips.

SERVE with dessert of your choice, if desired.

Main Dishes

Grilled Pork Chops with Hollandaise Sauce

12 center-cut pork chops,	Salt
1/2" thick (portion =	Pepper
2 per person)	2 c. Hollandaise Sauce
2 c. hot pepper relish	(recipe follows)

SEASON pork chops on both sides with salt and pepper. Charbroil or barbecue until fully cooked.

TOP each chop with 2 tablespoons Hollandaise Sauce and serve immediately.

HOLLANDAISE SAUCE:

1 3/4 c. butter, clarified from	1/4 tsp. Worcestershire sauce
2 lb. whole butter	Salt
6 egg yolks	Cayenne pepper
2 tsp. water	1 T. lemon juice, fresh

MELT butter in a double boiler or microwave. Do not allow butter to boil and do not stir while melting. Once melted, let butter stand 30 minutes while milk solids settle to bottom and foam rises to top. Top clarify butter, skim top and discard foam. Carefully remove yellow oil, leaving white milk solids on bottom of pan. Reserve only yellow oil part of butter. Keep warm, but not hot.

PLACE egg yolks in a stainless steel bowl with water and lemon juice. Place bowl over a pan of hot, not boiling, water and whisk egg yolks until pale yellow and foamy. Remove eggs from heat anytime they appear too hot, or they may scramble.

SLOWLY add clarified butter to eggs, in a steady stream, whipping after each addition. (Return eggs to hot water, while whipping, to help incorporate and thicken sauce.)

ADD butter slowly, or sauce could separate.

ADD more warm water to sauce if it becomes too thick.

THE final result should be like runny mayonnaise.

When all butter has been incorporated, add Worcestershire sauce and season with salt and cayenne pepper. Serve immediately.

SERVES 6.

THIS recipe may seem complicated, but if you follow the directions step-by-step, it is really not. The results are well worth the time.

Grilled Pork Medallions with Orange-Rosemary Glaze

1/2 c. white vinegar	2 tsp. chopped fresh rosemary,
1/4 c. sugar	or 1/2 tsp. dried
1 c. fresh orange juice	Salt & ground pepper, to taste
(about 3 oranges)	1 lb. pork tenderloin, trimmed
1 T. fresh lime juice	of fat & membrane & cut
(about 1/2 lime)	into 1"-thick slices

IN a small, heavy saucepan, combine vinegar and sugar. Boil, stirring occasionally, to dissolve the sugar. Reduce heat to medium and boil, without stirring, for 5 minutes. Add orange juice and boil for 20 to 25 minutes, or until the syrup is thick enough to coat the back of a wooden spoon. Remove from the heat and stir in lime juice, rosemary, salt and pepper; set aside.

PREPARE a charcoal or gas grill. Season pork with salt and pepper and grill on a lightly-oiled rack over medium-high heat for 2 to 3 minutes per side, or until the outside of the meat is brown. Brush with glaze.

YIELD: 4 servings.

Ham Loaf

3 c. soft bread crumbs	4 eggs, well beaten
1 1/2 c. milk	1/4 tsp. dry mustard
3 lb. ground ham	Salt & pepper, to taste
2 1/2 lb. ground hamburger	

MIX in order given.
BAKE 2 hours at 300°.

Herbed Pork Medallions
with Cheese
Chef Dave Bush

4 (4 oz.) boneless pork chops

MARINADE:

1 T. fresh garlic	1 tsp. fresh parsley
1 tsp. basil	1/4 c. olive oil
1 tsp. oregano	1 tsp. lemon juice
1 tsp. tarragon	1 pinch salt & black pepper

8 oz. heavy cream	1/2 c. fresh Parmesan cheese,
8 oz. cheese tortellini	grated

MAKE marinade and pour over chops. Let stand 2 hours.

IN a 10-inch sauté pan, cook pork chops until 155° internal temperature.

HEAT a separate 10-inch sauté pan. Add heavy cream and reduce over a high heat until it becomes creamy.

ADD cheese, and cheese tortellini.

PLACE cheese tortellini mixture, divided equally, in 2 bowls and top with pork medallions.

YIELD: 4 servings.

Honey-Glazed Ham

1 (10 to 12 lb.) finely-cooked bone-in ham	1/2 tsp. whole ginger
	3 (2") cinnamon sticks
2 c. apple juice or cider	1 c. honey
3/4 tsp. whole allspice	Whole cloves
1 tsp. cloves	Paprika

PLACE ham, fat-side up, on rack in shallow pan. Insert meat thermometer into center so it does not touch bone.

HEAT apple juice with allspice, 1 teaspoon whole cloves, ginger and stick cinnamon in saucepan, bringing to a boil. Cover and boil 5 minutes. Remove from heat and brush a little of this mixture over ham.

BAKE ham in slow oven (325°) for 1 1/2 to 2 hours, basting every 15 minutes with the spiced apple juice mixture.

DRIZZLE 1/2 cup honey over ham. Bake 30 minutes longer. Remove from oven and drizzle on remaining 1/2 cup honey. Bake 30 minutes, or until thermometer indicates internal temperature of 160°; about 15 minutes per pound.

REMOVE from oven and cool 30 minutes. Score fat, stud with whole cloves and sprinkle lavishly with paprika.

SERVE on platter.

GARNISH may be drained, spiced peaches on nests of parsley sprigs.

YIELD: 20 to 22 servings.

Honey Pork Loin Roast

4 lb. boneless pork loin
2 lg. apples, chopped
3 stalks celery, chopped
2 T. parsley
1 tsp. sage
Dash of salt
1 1/2 c. ketchup
1 c. honey
1/4 c. cooking oil
3 T. lemon juice
1 T. Worcestershire sauce

1/2 to 1 lb. butter or margarine
1 1/2 c. onions, chopped
1/2 loaf (about 10 slices)
 torn-up, toasted bread
1/4 tsp. pepper
1 2/3 c. barbecue sauce,
 hickory flavored
3/4 c. packed brown sugar
2 oz. brandy
1 T. prepared mustard

IN large skillet, melt butter; sauté apples, onions and celery. In a large bowl, mix bread, parsley, sage, pepper and salt.

COMBINE both mixtures and stir well. Cut a pocket in roast and stuff with filling mixture. Close flap and tie with cord.

IN a large bowl, mix rest of ingredients. Soak meat in this mixture for 2 to 4 hours.

REMOVE roast from mixture, retaining mixture.

PLACE roast, with mixture, in a roasting pan and bake at 325° for 2 to 2 1/2 hours, or until a meat thermometer registers 170°.

BASTE roast with mixture in roasting pan about every 1/2 hour.

TO SERVE, let roast stand for 10 minutes. Slice and place on meat platter, and serve with mixture.

THIS would be good served with baked potatoes and your choice of topping.

Jack Daniels Pork Tenderloin
Chef Bart Brockmann
2 lb. trimmed pork tenderloin

MARINADE:

4 c. heavy cream	1 oz. Jack Daniels bourbon
4 c. apple juice	1 tsp. salt
1 c. brown sugar	1 tsp. fresh ground pepper

CUT tenderloin into 4 (8-ounce) pieces.
MIX all 6 marinade ingredients in a bowl. Add pork and let marinate for 2 hours in your refrigerator.
REMOVE meat from marinade after 2 hours and keep cool until you're ready to grill. Reserve marinade.

SAUCE:
HEAT marinade in saucepan. Thicken with cornstarch and water mixture (2 teaspoons water mixed with 2 teaspoons cornstarch).

GRILL pork until done; until juices run clear and meat is no longer pink in the center.
YIELD: 4 servings.

Main Dishes

Make-Ahead Pork Tenderloin

8 (1 lb.) pork tenderloins,   1/3 c. olive oil (may use
  trimmed   vegetable)
1 T. grated fresh ginger root   1/4 c. parsley, minced, or 1/8 c.
  or 1/2 tsp. ground ginger   dried parsley
2 tsp. dried rosemary, crushed   2 tsp. dried oregano
1/2 tsp. salt (opt.)   1/2 tsp. paprika
1/4 tsp. ground nutmeg   1/4 tsp. pepper

PLACE tenderloins in an ungreased 9x13x2-inch glass baking dish.
COMBINE remaining ingredients; rub over tenderloins.
COVER and refrigerate 6 hours or overnight.
BAKE, uncovered, at 425° for 25 to 30 minutes, or until a meat
thermometer reads 160° to 170°. Let stand for 5 minutes before slicing.
YIELD: 8 servings.

THIS is a great meat for a quick meal. Prepare the night before, and it takes
such a short time to bake. Goes great with Refrigerator Potato Rolls.

Maple-Glazed Ribs

3 lb. pork spareribs, cut   1 T. Dijon mustard
  into serving-size pieces   1 T. Worcestershire sauce
1 c. maple syrup   1 tsp. curry powder
3 T. orange juice concentrate   1 garlic clove, minced
3 T. ketchup   2 green onions, minced
2 T. soy sauce   1 T. sesame seeds, toasted

PLACE ribs, meat side-up, on a rack in a greased 9x13x2-inch baking
pan. Cover pan tightly with foil.
BAKE at 350° for 1 1/4 hours.
MEANWHILE, combine the next 9 ingredients in a saucepan. Bring
to a boil over medium heat. Reduce heat; simmer for 15 minutes,
stirring occasionally.
DRAIN ribs. Remove rack and return ribs to pan. Cover with sauce.
BAKE, uncovered, for 35 minutes, basting occasionally.
SPRINKLE with sesame seeds just before serving.
YIELD: 6 servings.

Marinated Pork Loin Roast

3/4 c. ketchup
1/4 c. white wine vinegar
1/4 c. maple-flavored syrup
2 T. lemon juice
1 tsp. salt
1 tsp. pepper
1 bay leaf
1 boneless pork loin roast
  (3 lb.)

1/4 c. seedless raspberry jam
1/4 c. packed brown sugar
2 T. Worcestershire sauce
1 tsp. dried thyme
1 tsp. oregano
1 tsp. marjoram
1 tsp. Dijon mustard
1/4 tsp. ground ginger

IN a saucepan, combine all ingredients except pork. Bring to a boil over medium heat.

PLACE roast in a 7x11x2-inch baking dish. Using a fork, prick surface of roast; pour sauce over roast.

COVER and refrigerate overnight.

BAKE, uncovered, at 325° for 1 1/2 to 2 hours. Let stand 10 minutes before slicing. Remove bay leaf.

YIELD: 10 servings.

SERVE with Cinnamon Beans and Colorado Creme.

Medallions of Pork
with Three-Mustard Sauce
Chef Mike Reeh

1 T. butter	1 T. butter
4 (2 oz.) pork medallions	1 tsp. Dutch (Creole) mustard
Seasoned flour as needed	1 tsp. yellow mustard
(see recipe below)	1 T. Dijon mustard
1 T. sliced green onion	Dash of Tabasco
1 oz. brandy	1/4 tsp. fresh garlic, minced
8 oz. heavy cream	Salt & pepper, to taste

HEAT skillet with 1 tablespoon butter.

SEASON pork medallions with salt and pepper.

DREDGE pork medallions in seasoned flour.

SAUTÉ pork medallions until light brown on both sides.

REMOVE pork and place in warm spot.

ADD green onion to pan and flambé with brandy (handle flame with care).

ADD heavy cream and all other ingredients, except butter.

KEEP on high heat until it forms a nice sauce.

LAST, swirl in 1 tablespoon butter and serve over pork medallions.

YIELD: 4 servings.

SEASONED FLOUR:

1/2 c. flour	1 tsp. Chef Salt

CHEF SALT:

3 T. salt	1/2 tsp. white pepper
1/2 T. paprika	1/2 tsp. garlic salt
1/2 tsp. black pepper	1/2 tsp. onion salt

Mexican Spareribs

1 T. brown sugar
1 T. paprika
1 1/2 tsp. chili powder
3/4 tsp. salt
1/2 tsp. garlic powder

1 T. pepper
1 1/2 tsp. crushed red pepper flakes
3 lb. pork spareribs
3 (18"x40") sheets heavy-duty
   foil

COMBINE the first 7 ingredients; mix well. Rub ingredients onto both sides of ribs. Stack 3 sheets of foil together. Place ribs in the middle and fold foil down several times. Fold short ends toward the food, and crimp to prevent leaks.
REFRIGERATE overnight. Remove from refrigerator 30 minutes before grilling.
GRILL, covered, over indirect heat and medium-low coals, meat-side down, for 45 minutes.
TURN and cook 45 minutes more.
REMOVE ribs from foil and place on grill rack. Grill, uncovered, for 10 to 15 minutes, turning once.
YIELD: 4 servings.

YOU could grill fresh vegetables at the same time you place the ribs on the grill rack, and they would be done about the same time the ribs would be. RIBS are always good with fresh watermelon, and any fresh fruit pie of your choice.

Oriental Pork Ribs

2 c. tomato ketchup
1/4 c. soy sauce
1/4 c. pineapple juice
1/4 c. pineapple, fresh
1/4 c. orange juice, fresh

1/2 c. brown sugar
1 T. wine vinegar
3 whole cloves
1 tsp. orange rind, grated
Pork spareribs (1 lb. per person)

COMBINE all ingredients except ribs, and blend well. Allow mixture to stand in refrigerator overnight. Strain before using.
CUT ribs into serving-size pieces. Place on a rack in a roasting pan.
BAKE in preheated 275° oven, basting with sauce often, for 2 to 2 1/2 hours, or until meat separates easily from bone.
REFRIGERATE any leftover sauce.
YIELD: 3 cups sauce.

Main Dishes

Paprika Pork Roast

2 tsp. garlic salt	1 boneless rolled pork loin roast
1 tsp. ground ginger	(4 to 4 1/2 lb.)
1 tsp. pepper	1 to 2 med. onions, sliced
1 tsp. paprika	1 c. water

COMBINE salt, garlic, ginger, pepper and paprika; rub over the entire roast. Place roast, fat-side up, on a greased rack in a roasting pan.
BAKE, uncovered, at 325° for 2 to 2 1/2 hours, or until a meat thermometer reads 160 to 170°.
LET stand for 10 to 15 minutes before slicing.
YIELD: 8 to 10 servings.

SINCE this is a spicy roast, I like to keep the rest of my meal rather simple, such as Zucchini and Corn Sauté and Whipped Potatoes.

 ## Peppered Pork Loin
Chef Bart Brockmann

2 lb. boneless pork loin

SEASONINGS:	2 tsp. dried ground oregano
1 T. olive oil	1 1/2 tsp. pepper
1 T. garlic powder	1 tsp. salt
1 T. paprika	1 tsp. lemon pepper
2 tsp. dried ground thyme	1 tsp. ground red pepper

CUT pork loin into 4 (8-ounce) portions.
IN a bowl, combine all seasonings.
SPRINKLE seasonings over pork, and press into both sides.
COVER and chill for 1 hour.
GRILL pork until done; until juices run clear, and meat is no longer pink in center.
YIELD: 4 servings.

Peppered Rack of Pork

1 (4 to 5 lb.) center loin pork   2 cloves garlic, peeled
  roast, backbone removed   Coarsely-ground pepper
  (trim excess fat from loin
  & all extra meat from rib
  bones, or you may ask
  your butcher to "French"
  the bones)

PREHEAT oven to 350°.
CUT garlic cloves in half, and run over all surfaces of loin; sprinkle
generously with black pepper.
PLACE in shallow roasting pan, with bones up, and roast 60 to 90
minutes (about 18 to 20 minutes per pound) until meat thermometer
placed in center of loin eye reads about 155°.
REMOVE roast from oven; let rest 10 minutes.
CUT between rib bones to serve.
YIELD: 6 servings.

THIS roast is great hot, but very good to take sliced to serve with
potato salad, tomatoes, etc., at a picnic.

Pork and Pepper Supper

This is a great meal in the summer with all fresh vegetables, but still good even in winter with frozen.

MARINADE:

2 fresh limes	1/2 tsp. thyme leaves
1/4 c. soy sauce	Dash of cayenne pepper
1/2 tsp. bay leaves	4 cloves garlic, crushed
1/2 tsp. oregano leaves	2 to 3 fresh parsley sprigs (opt.)

PORK:

1 lb. pork tenderloin, trimmed, 1" cubes	2 med. tomatoes, cut into 8 pieces, seeded
1 T. olive oil	1 lg. green pepper, cut into 8 pieces
1 tsp. brown sugar	
2 med. onions, cut into 8 pieces	1 lg. red pepper, cut into 8 pieces

SQUEEZE juice from limes, reserving peel. In a small bowl, combine all marinade ingredients, including lime peel; blend well.

PLACE pork cubes in resealable plastic bag or shallow glass dish.

POUR marinade over pork, turning to coat.

SEAL bag or cover dish; marinate at least 2 hours, or overnight, in refrigerator, turning pork several times.

REMOVE lime peel, parsley and bay leaf from marinade; discard.

REMOVE pork from marinade, reserving marinade.

DRAIN pork well.

HEAT oil in a large skillet over high heat. Add brown sugar. Stir until sugar is brown and bubbly.

ADD pork cubes. Cook and stir about 5 minutes or until pork is browned.

REDUCE heat to low; add onions, tomatoes, peppers and reserved marinade.

SIMMER 10 to 15 minutes.

SERVE over rice or egg noodles.

YIELD: 4 servings.

Main Dishes 163

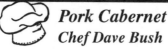

Pork Cabernet
Chef Dave Bush

4 (2 oz.) medallions of pork
1/2 c. seasoned flour
   (see recipe below)
1 T. finely-diced onion
1/4 c. peeled, seeded
   tomatoes
1/4 c. sliced mushrooms

1 T. green onion
1 tsp. chopped parsley
1/4 c. Cabernet Sauvignon
1 oz. butter, to sauté
Chef Salt, to taste
   (see recipe below)
4 oz. beef gravy

CUT and pound medallions from pork tenderloin.
HEAT butter in sauté pan.
DREDGE pork in flour and place in sauté pan.
SAUTÉ pork for about 2 minutes on each side, to medium-well (about 155°).
REMOVE pork from pan and add onion, mushrooms, green onion, chopped parsley and gravy.
COOK until most of the liquid evaporates, and add beef gravy.
HEAT thoroughly and serve over pork.
YIELD: 4 servings.

SEASONED FLOUR:
1/2 c. flour
1 tsp. Chef Salt

CHEF SALT:
3 T. salt
1/2 T. paprika
1/2 tsp. black pepper

1/2 tsp. white pepper
1/2 tsp. garlic salt
1/2 tsp. onion salt

Main Dishes

Pork Chops, Cajun

4 tsp. paprika	2 tsp. salt
2 tsp. rubbed sage	3/4 tsp. cayenne pepper
3/4 tsp. pepper	3/4 tsp. garlic powder
4 butterfly pork chops	2 T. butter or margarine
(1 1/2" thick)	

IN a shallow bowl, combine the spices. Dip each chop into the seasoning mixture and press into both sides.

IN a heavy skillet, heat butter on high until browned. Reduce heat to medium; cook the chops for 2 to 3 minutes per side or until browned and juices run clear.

YIELD: 4 servings.

Pork Cutlets with Pepper Spices

1 (1 lb.) pork tenderloin	1 tsp. dried thyme
1 tsp. paprika	1/2 tsp. dried oregano
1/4 tsp. salt	1/2 tsp. dried rosemary, crushed
1/4 tsp. ground white pepper	1/4 tsp. black pepper
1 tsp. ground red pepper	1 tsp. olive oil
2 cloves garlic, crushed	Vegetable cooking spray

CUT pork crosswise into 12 slices. Place each pork slice between 2 sheets of heavy-duty plastic wrap and flatten to 1/4-inch thickness, using the heel of your hand or a meat mallet.

COMBINE paprika and the next 9 ingredients; rub over both sides of pork slices. Place pork on a broiler rack coated with cooking spray; place rack in a broiler pan. Broil 5 1/2 inches from heat (with electric oven door partially open), 3 to 4 minutes on each side or until done.

YIELD: 4 servings.

THIS would be a really fast meal to prepare; you could serve with steamed broccoli spears, pork-flavored rice and ice cream.

Pork Filet Mignon

9 lean pork chops, boned,
    1" thick; or 9 pork
    tenderloin slices, 1" thick
9 slices bacon

9 lg. whole mushrooms,
    stemmed
3 T. butter

SHAPE boned chops into rounds; circle each with a strip of bacon and secure with toothpicks.

PLACE in flat baking dish and cover.

BAKE in 300° oven for 1 hour.

UNCOVER; brown under broiler.

SAUTÉ mushrooms in butter until brown and tender.

TOP each fillet with a mushroom.

YIELD: 9 servings.

THIS recipe may be grilled.

Pork Kabobs

1 1/2 lb. boneless pork,
    cut into 3/4" cubes
1 med. zucchini, cut into
    1" slices
1 c. molasses
2/3 c. soy sauce

1 med. sweet red pepper, cut
    into 1" pieces
12 lg. fresh mushrooms
1 (20 oz.) can pineapple
    chunks in juice, undrained

PLACE pork, peppers, zucchini and mushrooms in a large resealable plastic bag, or shallow glass container.

DRAIN the pineapple, reserving 1/2 cup of the juice. Add pineapple chunks to pork mixture.

COMBINE molasses, soy sauce and pineapple juice; mix well. Reserve 1/2 cup for basting, and refrigerate.

POUR remaining sauce over meat and vegetables. Seal bag, or if using a glass container, cover; refrigerate for several hours. Drain, and discard marinade.

ON 12 metal or soaked bamboo skewers, alternate pork, vegetables and pineapple.

GRILL, uncovered, over medium coals, turning and basting with reserved marinade, for 12 to 15 minutes or until juices run clear.

YIELD: 6 servings (12 kabobs).

THESE are good served with a fresh fruit salad, and a light sherbet with coconut macaroon cookies.

Pork Ribs - Country-Style

4 lb. country-style pork ribs

VINEGAR BASTING SAUCE:

2/3 c. water   1/3 c. red wine vinegar

PLACE ribs in a shallow roasting pan; pour basting sauce over ribs.
COVER with aluminum foil and bake for 1 hour at 300°, basting with
vinegar mixture halfway through cooking time.
DRAIN ribs, discarding basting sauce.
GRILL over low coals for 15 minutes, turning after 8 minutes. Baste
heavily with barbecue sauce (below), and grill another 7 minutes.
YIELD: 4 to 8 servings

BARBECUE SAUCE:

1 c. ketchup	1 c. water
1/2 c. cider vinegar	1/3 c. Worcestershire sauce
1/4 c. prepared mustard	1/4 c. butter or margarine
1/2 c. firmly-packed brown	1 tsp. hot sauce
sugar	1/8 tsp. salt

COMBINE all ingredients in a saucepan, stirring well. Bring to a boil.
Cover, reduce heat, and simmer 1 hour.
YIELD: 3 cups.

THESE ribs would taste great with coleslaw and corn on the cob, or
frozen whole kernel corn.

Pork Ribs with Barbecue Sauce

1 lb. ribs per person

1 c. tomato ketchup
1 c. chili sauce
1/2 c. currant jelly
1/4 c. Dijon mustard
1/2 c. brown sugar
1 T. Worcestershire sauce
1 tsp. dry mustard

1/4 c. honey
1 tsp. black pepper, coarsely
   cracked
Salt
1/4 c. red wine vinegar
2 T. steak sauce

COMBINE above ingredients and blend well.
CUT ribs into serving-size pieces and cover with barbecue sauce.
MARINATE in refrigerator for several hours or overnight.
GRILL ribs over low coals for about 1 hour, basting occasionally with
additional sauce. Turn ribs frequently.
REFRIGERATE any additional sauce.
YIELD: 3 1/2 cups sauce.

Pork Scaloppine with Wine

2 (3/4 lb.) pork tenderloins
1/4 c. butter or margarine,
   divided
2 tsp. beef-flavored bouillon
   granules

1/8 tsp. freshly-ground pepper
1/2 c. all-purpose flour
1 1/3 c. dry Marsala, or 1 1/4 c.
   dry white wine
Hot cooked rice

CUT each tenderloin into 6 (2-ounce) medallions. Place pork, cut-side down, between 2 sheets of heavy-city plastic wrap. Flatten to 1/4-inch thickness, using meat mallet or rolling pin,

DREDGE pork in flour. Cook half of pork medallions in 2 tablespoons butter in a large skillet over medium heat, about 2 minutes on each side, or until lightly browned.

REMOVE from skillet; keep warm. Repeat procedure with remaining 2 tablespoons butter and pork medallions. Pour off excess butter, if necessary, leaving pan drippings.

ADD wine, bouillon granules and pepper to skillet, and simmer mixture 3 to 4 minutes.

RETURN pork medallions to skillet. Cover and simmer 2 minutes.

SERVE with rice.

YIELD: 6 servings.

THIS is actually a rather quick meal to make, just add your favorite vegetable and dessert, and you can be ready to eat within 1 hour or less.

Pork Tenderloin with Green Apples and Peppercorns

1 lb. pork tenderloin, trimmed	1 tart apple, unpeeled, cored &
3/4 tsp. poultry seasoning	cut into 1/4" slices
2 to 4 tsp. crushed green	1/2 tsp. garlic salt
peppercorns	1/4 tsp. nutmeg
3 T. apple juice concentrate,	1 T. margarine
thawed	1 T. cornstarch
1/2 c. dry white wine	1/2 c. chicken broth
Seedless red grapes (opt.)	1 T. vegetable oil

CUT pork tenderloin crosswise into 1/2-inch slices.

IN small bowl, combine garlic salt, poultry seasoning and nutmeg. Sprinkle seasoning mixture over each pork slice; coat both sides lightly with peppercorns.

HEAT margarine in 12-inch skillet over medium-high heat. Add apple slices; cook 3 to 4 minutes or until crisp-tender. Remove apples; set aside.

HEAT oil in same skillet over medium heat. Add pork slices; brown about 2 minutes per side. Remove pork from skillet.

IN small bowl, dissolve cornstarch in apple juice concentrate. Add to same skillet; stir in wine and broth. Bring to a boil, stirring constantly.

RETURN pork slices to skillet; reduce heat to low. Cover and simmer 10 minutes or until pork is tender.

PLACE pork on serving plate. Top with apple wedges; spoon wine mixture over pork and apples.

GARNISH with grapes, if desired.

YIELD: 4 servings.

BAKED RICE:	1 green pepper
1 stick margarine	2 cans beef consommé
1 onion, chopped	1 c. rice

BROWN onion, pepper and margarine. Add consommé and rice; cook for 10 minutes on medium heat.

PLACE in sprayed casserole dish and bake for 1 hour at 350°.

Pork Tenderloin with Mustard Sauce

MARINADE:

1/4 c. soy sauce	2 T. brown sugar
1/4 c. bourbon	3 lb. pork tenderloin

MUSTARD SAUCE:

2/3 c. sour cream	2 T. dry mustard
2/3 c. mayonnaise	3 or 4 green onions, chopped

COMBINE soy sauce, bourbon and brown sugar in a 7 x 11 x 1 1/2-inch baking dish. Add tenderloin.

MARINATE in refrigerate for at least 2 hours, turning tenderloin occasionally.

PREPARE sauce by combining sour cream, mayonnaise, mustard and onion. Chill for at least 1 hour.

REMOVE tenderloin from marinade and place on rack in shallow roasting pan.

BAKE at 325° for 45 minutes, or until internal temperature is 160°.

SERVE with mustard sauce.

YIELD: 8 servings.

THIS goes great with Fried Cauliflower Au Gratin.

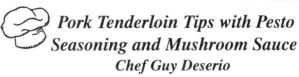

Pork Tenderloin Tips with Pesto Seasoning and Mushroom Sauce
Chef Guy Deserio

2 lb. trimmed (silver skin removed) pork tenderloin

ADD:
1 oz. olive oil   4 oz. pesto

SAUTÉ meat; set aside, keep warm.

MUSHROOM SAUCE:
1 1/2 c. brown gravy   1 tsp. garlic, minced
1/2 c. Merlot wine   2 tsp. water mixed with 2 tsp.
1 c. sliced, sautéed mushrooms   cornstarch

DEGLAZE pan with Merlot wine.
ADD Mushroom Sauce and minced garlic; cook about 5 to 8 minutes to reduce some of the liquid.
ADD the cornstarch and water mixture, stirring constantly, allow to thicken.
POUR sauce over pork.

PESTO:
3 1/2 oz. basil (about 1/2 c.)   1 fluid oz. olive oil
fresh basil (dry basil,   2 oz. Parmesan cheese (1/4 c.)
1/4 c.)   2 tsp. garlic
2 1/2 oz. (1/3 c.) pine nuts, or 4 tsp. water
almonds (opt.) (1/3 c.)

BLEND all ingredients together in food processor. Process for 30 seconds to 1 minute.
YIELD: 4 servings.

NOTE from Chef Guy Deserio: "This recipe is always popular with my cooking classes. It works equally well with beef or pork. I like it served over wild rice with roasted vegetables."

Main Dishes   **173**

Pork with Jack Daniels
Apple Butter
Chef Mike Reeh

3 (2 oz.) pork cutlets   1 oz. Jack Daniels whiskey
1 T. butter   2 oz. butter
2 T. flour   Pinch of Chef Salt, to taste
1 tsp. finely-chopped onions   (see recipe below)
1/4 c. diced or sliced apples   1 tsp. sugar

CUT pork cutlets from boneless pork loin.
HEAT butter in 10-inch skillet; dredge pork cutlets in the 2 table-spoons flour and sauté about 2 to 3 minutes on each side.
REMOVE pork from skillet; set aside.
ADD chopped onion, apples and sugar to pan; sauté.
FLAME with Jack Daniels (being very careful with flame), and quickly shake in butter. Serve over pork cutlets.

CHEF'S SALT:
3 T. salt   1/2 tsp. white pepper
1/2 T. paprika   1/2 tsp. garlic salt
1/2 tsp. black pepper   1/2 tsp. onion salt

Roast Pork Loaf and Garcia Sauce
Chef Nicholas Garcia

2 lb. pork tenderloin,
   trimmed

CUT pork into 4 (8-ounce) pieces. Sauté in 1 tablespoon butter for 2 to 3 minutes on each side. Set aside; keep warm.

1/2 c. butter
1 1/2 c. onions or shallots,
   1/4" diced
1 1/2 oz. fresh garlic, finely
   chopped
1/2 c. tomato purée
1 c. white wine

6 c. brown gravy (if you have
   access to a restaurant
   supply, you may want to
   look for Demi Glace, and
   use that instead of gravy)
2 tsp. tarragon, chopped 1/8"
2 tsp. chervil, chopped 1/8"
1 c. mushrooms, sliced

IN a skillet or brasier, heat the butter; add onions (or shallots) and sauté until tender.
ADD garlic and sauté for 4 to 6 minutes.
ADD white wine and cook for 5 to 10 minutes.
ADD tomato purée; mix well.
ADD mushrooms and sauté for 3 minutes.
ADD tarragon and chervil; mix well.
ADD brown gravy (or Demi Glace); cook for 5 to 10 minutes.
TO serve, pour sauce over pork tenderloin.
YIELD: 4 servings.

Sausage-Cheese Fettuccine Primavera

1 lb. sausage, ground
2 garlic cloves, minced
1 T. flour
1/2 tsp. dried oregano leaves

1/2 tsp. coarse-grind pepper
1 med. onion, chopped
1 T. olive oil
1 tsp. dried basil leaves

BROWN sausage in heavy skillet; drain. Return to skillet and add oil, onions and garlic; sauté.
BLEND in flour and seasonings. Gradually add milk; cook, stirring constantly, until thickened.

PASTA:

1 3/4 c. skim milk
1 c. (4 oz.) Mozzarella
  cheese
2 c. broccoli flowerets,
  cooked & drained

8 oz. fettuccine, cooked &
  drained
2 T. grated Parmesan cheese
1 red pepper, cut into julienne
  strips

TOSS the hot pasta mixture with the sausage mixture and serve immediately.
YIELD: 4 servings.

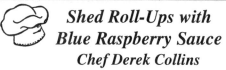

Shed Roll-Ups with Blue Raspberry Sauce
Chef Derek Collins

2 lb. center-cut pork loin

CUTTING MEAT: Begin by placing pork loin, silver-side down, with the pork lengthwise away from you. Then cut pork about an inch from the top, lengthwise away from you; do not cut all the way through. THEN, lay open pork like a butterfly.
CUT a straight line down the crease, then continue the same process to butterfly pork loin again, the other way.
PLACE pork aside in refrigerator.

FRUIT FILLING:
1/2 c. strawberries, diced small	1/2 c. cantaloupe, diced small
1/2 c. fresh blueberries	1/2 c. raspberries (you may use
1/2 c. pineapple, diced small	raspberry pie filling)

COMBINE all fruit with sugar. Allow to set-up for about 1/2 hour.

ROLLING PORK: Lay pork flat. Spread fruit filling evenly over loin. Start rolling pork carefully, so as not to allow filling to fall out. After loin is totally rolled, tie the loin securely with kitchen twine in 2-inch intervals. Lay loin on cookie sheet, with folded seam down. Season pork with 1 tablespoon garlic salt, sage and black pepper. Cook for 1 hour and 15 minutes, or until internal temperature is 160°.

BLUE RASPBERRY SAUCE:
1 qt. water (4 c.)	2 T. pork base
2 c. blueberries	1 tsp. fresh garlic
1 c. raspberries	1 c. sugar
1 onion, diced	2 c. heavy cream
1 carrot, sliced large	

ROUX:
1/4 lb. butter	1/4 lb. flour

COMBINE the first 7 ingredients in a saucepan on medium to high heat; bring to a boil.
REDUCE heat to low until carrots are tender.
STRAIN mixture into a bowl (make sure there are no pieces in liquid).
RETURN liquid to another saucepan and add sugar and heavy cream, on medium heat, bring back to a boil and add roux.

Main Dishes

Skillet Pork Chops

6 (4 oz.) boneless pork chops, trimmed
1 (10 3/4 oz.) can condensed golden mushroom soup, undiluted
2 tsp. Dijon mustard
1/4 tsp. salt
2 T. water
1 (14 1/2 oz.) can diced tomatoes, undrained
1/3 c. chopped onion
1 lb. fresh mushrooms, sliced
3 c. hot cooked rice or cooked noodles

COAT a skillet with nonstick cooking spray. Brown pork chops on both sides. Remove and set aside.

ADD water, scraping bottom of the skillet to loosen any browned bits.

DRAIN tomatoes, reserving juice; set tomatoes aside.

ADD juice, soup, onion, mustard, mushrooms and salt to skillet; mix well. Return chops to skillet.

COVER and simmer for 30 minutes, or until pork is tender. Stir in tomatoes; heat through.

COMBINE rice (or noodles) and parsley.

SERVE chops and sauce over rice (or noodles).

YIELD: 6 servings.

THIS is great served with Sunshine Carrots.

Sour Cream Ham Loaf

1 lb. fully-cooked ham, ground	1 lb. lean pork sausage
2 c. soft bread crumbs	2 eggs
1 c. (8 oz.) sour cream	1/3 c. chopped onion
2 T. lemon juice	1 tsp. curry powder
1 tsp. ground ginger	1 tsp. ground mustard
1/8 tsp. ground nutmeg	1/8 tsp. paprika

IN a large bowl, combine ham, sausage and bread crumbs.
IN a small bowl, beat eggs; add sour cream, onion, lemon juice and seasonings. Mix well; blend into meat mixture. Shape into a 9x5x2-inch loaf in greased, shallow baking pan.
BAKE, uncovered, at 350° for 30 minutes.

SAUCE:

1 c. packed brown sugar	1/2 c. water
1/2 c. cider vinegar	1/4 tsp. pepper

IN a small saucepan, combine sauce ingredients; bring to a boil. Pour over loaf.
BAKE, uncovered, 20 to 30 minutes longer, or until meat thermometer registers 160° to 170°, basting every 10 minutes.
LET stand 10 minutes before slicing.
YIELD: 6 to 8 servings.

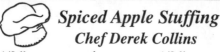
Spiced Apple Stuffing
Chef Derek Collins

1 1/2 lb. unseasoned croutons	1/2 lb. margarine
1 can apple rings, diced in	4 c. pork stock
1/4" pieces	1/2 c. roasted pecans
1 med. onion, diced	(see recipe below)
1 bunch celery, diced	

IN a large stockpot, add margarine, celery and onion. Sauté on medium heat until tender.
ADD pork stock and allow to heat to 150°; add remaining ingredients.
STIR until all is incorporated and croutons are tender, not wet.

ROASTED PECANS: Preheat oven to 350°.
PLACE pecans on a cookie sheet.
BAKE in oven about 5 minutes, or until pecans are golden brown.

SWEET RUM SAUCE:

1/2 qt. apple juice (1 c.)	1 c. brown sugar
1/2 qt. heavy cream (1 c.)	1 tsp. vanilla
2 oz. Meyers dark rum	1/4 c. roasted pecans

ROUX:

1/4 lb. butter	1/4 lb. flour

COMBINE the first 5 items in a saucepan on medium-high heat until it comes to a boil.
COMBINE the last 2 items and whisk in until it is smooth and creamy.

ROUX: In a saucepan, add butter and allow to melt; add flour. Mix well.

4 (10 oz.) bone-in pork chops

BUY at store from butcher.
IN a 275° oven, slow-roast pork for 20 to 25 minutes. Pork's internal temperature should be 155°.
REMOVE chop and slice down center of chop and fold open-face and stuff with stuffing. Then, fold meat back over and ribbon with Sweet Rum Sauce.

Main Dishes

Spicy Ham Steak

1/3 c. spicy brown mustard	1 fully-cooked ham steak
1/4 c. honey	(about 2 lb.)
1/2 tsp. grated orange peel	

IN a small bowl, combine mustard, honey and orange peel. Brush over one side of ham.

BROIL or grill, uncovered, over medium-hot heat for 7 minutes.

TURN; brush with mustard mixture.

COOK until well glazed and heated through, about 7 minutes.

YIELD: 6 to 8 servings.

THIS is a great fast meal, you could serve with a Tomato-Cucumber Salad, Potato Salad, and a Quick Ice Cream Pie.

Stir-Fried Pork with Cauliflower and Broccoli

1/4 c. blanched almonds or
   cashews, coarsely
   chopped (opt.)
2 T. soy sauce
4 tsp. cornstarch
2 tsp. sesame oil
3/4 lb. pork tenderloin,
   trimmed
1 sm. bunch cauliflower, cut
   into florets
1 red bell pepper, seeded &
   thinly sliced

1 T. peeled, minced ginger root
2 T. chicken stock, defatted
1 T. rice-wine vinegar
2 tsp. sugar
1 sm. bunch broccoli, cut into
   florets
1 T. vegetable oil
4 scallions, thinly sliced
1 clove garlic, minced
1 jalapeño pepper, with seeds,
   minced
Salt & pepper, to taste

IF using almonds or cashews, preheat oven to 350°. Spread nuts on a pie plate and toast for 8 to 10 minutes, or until lightly browned.

IN A small bowl, mix together soy sauce, chicken stock, 1 tablespoon cornstarch, vinegar, sesame oil and sugar; set aside.

CUT pork in half lengthwise, then into very thin slices. Sprinkle with the remaining 1 teaspoon cornstarch, rubbing it in well.

BLANCH broccoli and cauliflower in boiling, salted water for 2 to 3 minutes, or just until tender-crisp. Drain, pat dry and set aside.

IN a wok or a large nonstick skillet, heat 1 teaspoon vegetable oil over high heat until hot, but not smoking. Add half the pork and stir-fry for 1 to 2 minutes, or until no longer pink outside. Remove and set aside. Stir-fry bell peppers until just tender, about 30 seconds. Add to the pork.

ADD the remaining 1 teaspoon oil. Add scallions, garlic, chili peppers and ginger; stir-fry for about 15 seconds. Return pork and peppers to the pan, and add broccoli, cauliflower and soy sauce mixture. Stir-fry until the sauce has thickened, about 1 minute. Season with salt and pepper to taste. If using nuts, sprinkle them over top and serve with rice.

YIELD: 4 servings.

Main Dishes

Stuffed Crown Pork Roast

1 pork crown rib roast   1 tsp. salt
   (about 6 lb.)   1 tsp. dried thyme
3 T. all-purpose flour   1/4 tsp. pepper
1 tsp. dried parsley flakes

RUB the inside and outside of roast with salt. Combine the flour, thyme, parsley and pepper; rub over outside of roast.
PLACE roast, with rib ends down, in a large roasting pan.
BAKE at 325° for 2 hours.

STUFFING:
1 lg. onion, chopped   3 T. cooking oil
4 c. coarsely-chopped fresh   4 c. chopped fresh broccoli
   mushrooms   1/2 tsp. chicken bouillon
3/4 tsp. salt   granules
1/4 tsp. dried thyme   1/4 tsp. pepper
6 c. onion & sage stuffing   1/2 c. water
   mix

IN a skillet, sauté onion in oil until tender. Add mushrooms, broccoli, salt, bouillon, thyme and pepper; cook for 8 minutes or until broccoli is crisp-tender. Stir in stuffing mix and water.
TURN roast over, with rib-ends up; fill center of roast with about 3 cups stuffing.
BAKE 1 hour longer, or until meat thermometer reads 160° to 170°. Bake remaining stuffing in a greased, covered baking dish during the last 40 minutes of baking time.
TRANSFER roast to serving platter; let stand 15 minutes before slicing.

GRAVY: 1/8 to 1/4 tsp. pepper
3 T. all-purpose flour   1/2 tsp. salt

Continued on following page.

Continued from preceding page.

DRAIN drippings into a measuring cup; skim and discard fat. Add enough water to drippings to measure 3 cups; stir in flour.
POUR into skillet, stirring to loosen browned bits. Add salt and pepper. Bring to a boil over medium heat; boil for 2 minutes, stirring constantly.
SERVE with roast and stuffing.
YIELD: 12 servings.

YOU may make any stuffing you prefer. Sweet dressing is always very good with pork.
MASHED potatoes are always good with gravy; you could try a new variation and add a little sour cream and chives when you mash the potatoes.
THIS roast is great with any accompanying vegetable, salad, rolls and desserts that are your favorites.

Stuffed Pork Chops

1 1/2 c. chopped fresh mushrooms	4 green onions, finely chopped
1/3 c. finely-chopped celery	1 T. butter or margarine
1 sm. tomato, chopped	1/4 to 1/2 tsp. dried marjoram
1/8 to 1/4 tsp. garlic salt	1/8 tsp. pepper
2 slices day-old white bread, cut into 1/4" cubes	4 pork chops (1" to 1 1/2" thick)

IN a skillet over medium heat, sauté mushrooms, onions and celery in butter until tender. Add the tomato, marjoram, garlic salt and pepper; cook and stir for 5 minutes.
REMOVE from the heat and stir in bread cubes.
CUT a large pocket in the side of each chop. Stuff mushroom mixture into pockets.
PLACE chops in an ungreased, shallow baking pan.
BAKE, uncovered, at 350° for 1 hour, or until juices run clear.
YIELD: 4 servings.

Main Dishes

Sweet and Sour Pork

1 med. onion, sliced into thin wedges	1 sm. green pepper, thinly sliced
1 clove garlic, minced	1 sm. red pepper, thinly sliced
1 lb. pork loin	2 T. cooking oil, divided
3 T. cornstarch	2 (8 oz.) cans unsweetened pineapple chunks, undrained
1/2 c. corn syrup	
3 T. soy sauce	1/4 c. vinegar
Hot cooked rice	2 T. ketchup

IN a large skillet or wok over medium-high heat, stir-fry onion, peppers and garlic in 1 tablespoon oil for 3 to 4 minutes, or until crisp-tender. Remove vegetables; set aside and keep warm.

CUT pork into 3 x 1/2 x 1/8-inch strips; stir-fry over medium-high heat in remaining oil for 5 to 7 minutes, or until no longer pink.

DRAIN pineapple, reserving juice; set pineapple aside. Combine juice and cornstarch. Add corn syrup, vinegar, soy sauce and ketchup. Add to skillet with vegetables and pineapple.

BRING to a boil; boil and stir for 2 minutes.

SERVE over rice.

YIELD: 4 servings.

WHEN I make this recipe, I usually vary it by adding sliced carrots. FOR DESSERT: I like to serve something very simple, like ice cream, either a simple ice cream pie, or ice cream sundaes.

Sweet and Sour Pork Chops

1/2 c. mayonnaise	1/4 c. prepared mustard
1/4 c. packed brown sugar	1/3 c. red wine vinegar
2 tsp. seasoned salt	4 pork chops (1" thick)

COMBINE the mayonnaise, brown sugar, seasoned salt and mustard; mix well. Blend in vinegar. Pour into resealable plastic bag or shallow glass dish; add pork. Seal bag or cover container; refrigerate overnight.

DRAIN and discard marinade. Grill, covered, over medium coals, turning occasionally, for 20 to 25 minutes or until juices run clear.

YIELD: 4 servings.

Sweet Pork Ribs

1 lg. onion, sliced
3 to 3 1/2 lb. country-style
   pork ribs
3 garlic cloves, minced
1/4 tsp. salt
1/2 c. water, divided
1/2 tsp. ground mustard

1 (20 oz.) can crushed
   pineapple in juice,
   undrained
1 (12 oz.) btl. chili sauce
1/2 c. packed brown sugar
1/4 tsp. pepper
1 tsp. ground ginger

PLACE onion in a 9x13x2-inch baking dish.

RUB ribs with garlic and sprinkle with salt and pepper; place over onion.

POUR 1/4 cup water around ribs.

COVER and bake at 350° for 30 minutes.

COMBINE pineapple, chili sauce, brown sugar, ginger, mustard and remaining water.

DRAIN fat from pan; pour pineapple mixture over ribs.

BAKE, uncovered, 1 1/2 hours longer, or until meat is tender.

YIELD: 6 servings.

DESSERTS

List Your Favorite Recipes

Recipes   **Page**

_____   _____

_____   _____

_____   _____

_____   _____

_____   _____

_____   _____

_____   _____

_____   _____

_____   _____

_____   _____

_____   _____

_____   _____

_____   _____

_____   _____

_____   _____

Apple-Cheese Crisp

6 c. peeled, cored & sliced
    cooking apples
1 c. (4 oz.) shredded Cheddar
    cheese
2 T. sugar
1/4 tsp. ground nutmeg
Vanilla ice cream
1 T. water

1/2 tsp. lemon juice
1 c. all-purpose flour
1/2 c. firmly-packed brown
    sugar
1/4 c. ground cinnamon
1/2 c. butter or margarine
Toasted almonds (opt.)

ARRANGE apple slices in a lightly-greased 8-inch square baking dish.

COMBINE water and lemon juice; sprinkle evenly over apple slices. Top evenly with cheese.

COMBINE flour and next 4 ingredients; cut in butter with pastry blender until mixture is crumbly. Sprinkle over cheese.

BAKE at 350° for 40 minutes, or until tender. Serve warm, topped with vanilla ice cream; sprinkle with almonds, if desired.

YIELD: 6 to 8 servings.

Apple Pancake Dessert

1/2 c. flour	3 T. sugar
1/2 tsp. baking soda	1/4 tsp. ground cinnamon
1/4 tsp. ground allspice	1 egg, lightly beaten
1/4 c. 1% milk	1 tsp. salad oil
1 tsp. lemon juice	1 c. peeled, shredded apples,
Pan spray	slightly packed
2 T. brown sugar	1/4 c. sour cream

IN a medium bowl, combine flour, sugar, baking soda and spices; stir until well blended. Beat egg with milk and oil. Sprinkle lemon juice over shredded apple.

COMBINE egg mixture with shredded apples, and mix. Stir apple and flour mixtures together until blended.

HEAT a 10-inch nonstick sauté pan over medium heat. Spray, and add apple batter. Cook over low to medium heat until just brown on the bottom, and sides begin to firm, 5 to 7 minutes.

FLIP pancake and continue to cook over low heat until browned and it springs back from finger touch, about 5 minutes.

REMOVE from heat and slide onto a plate. Top with chopped almonds and a dollop of sour cream; sprinkle with brown sugar.

SERVE with ice cream of your choice.

Baked Pears with Ice Cream

2 (16 oz.) cans pear halves,	1 c. crumbled coconut
drained	macaroons or amaretti
1/2 c. honey	cookies
1/4 c. butter or margarine,	Vanilla ice cream
melted	

ARRANGE pear halves in a 7 x 11 x 1 1/2-inch baking dish.
COMBINE honey and butter; pour over pears.
BAKE, uncovered, at 350° for 20 minutes.
SPRINKLE crumbled cookies over pears; bake 10 more minutes.
SERVE warm with ice cream.
YIELD: 6 servings.

Banana Split Pie

1 (9") frozen deep-dish
  pastry shell
1 (8 oz.) pkg. cream cheese,
  softened
1 c. sifted powdered sugar
1/2 c. crunchy peanut butter

1/2 c. chocolate syrup
2 c. frozen whipped topping,
  thawed
2 ripe bananas, mashed
Additional chocolate syrup
Maraschino cherries (opt.)

BAKE pastry shell according to package directions; let cool.
BEAT cream cheese at medium speed of an electric mixer until fluffy.
Add powdered sugar and peanut butter; beating until blended. Gradually add 1/2 cup chocolate syrup, beating well. Fold in whipped topping and mashed banana.
SPOON filling into pastry shell. Cover and freeze pie for 8 hours. Let stand at room temperature for 20 minutes before serving.
DRIZZLE each serving with additional chocolate syrup, and top with cherries, if desired.
YIELD: 8 servings.

Blackberry Crumb Pie

1 c. sugar
1 (8 oz.) ctn. sour cream
3 T. all-purpose flour
1/8 tsp. salt
4 c. fresh blackberries

1 unbaked 9-inch pastry shell
1 T. sugar
1/4 c. fine, dry bread crumbs
1 T. sugar
1 T. butter or margarine, melted

COMBINE the first 4 ingredients; stir well. Place blackberries in unbaked pastry shell; sprinkle 1 tablespoon sugar over berries.
SPREAD sour cream mixture over berries.
COMBINE bread crumbs, 1 tablespoon sugar and butter; sprinkle over top.
BAKE at 375° for 45 to 50 minutes, or until center of pie is firm.
YIELD: 1 (9-inch) pie.

YOU may use blueberries in place of blackberries.

Boston Cream Pie for Dessert

2 egg yolks	1 1/2 c. whole milk
1 1/2 T. flour	1 T. butter
1 T. cornstarch	1/2 c. whipping cream
1/4 c. powdered sugar	1 tsp. vanilla

BEAT the yolks in a double boiler; stir in flour, cornstarch, sugar, milk and butter.

COOK over boiling water about 20 minutes, until thick, stirring constantly.

CHILL mixture. When cold, whip the cream with the vanilla and fold together.

REFRIGERATE.

CAKE section: Any two layers of sponge cake or pound cake.

CHOCOLATE ICING:

2 sq. unsweetened	1 egg
· chocolate (2 oz.)	3/4 c. powdered sugar
3 T. cream	1 T. water & 1/2 tsp. vanilla

MELT chocolate in top of double boiler, remove from heat.

BEAT in sugar and water at once. Add yolk and beat well. Beat in cream, 1 tablespoon at a time, then vanilla.

PUT the cream filling between cake layers.

SPREAD the chocolate over the top, allowing some to drizzle over edges. Keep refrigerated.

Brownie Cake

1 pkg. fudge brownie mix	1/2 c. pecans
1/3 c. water	1 1/2 c. whipping cream
1/4 c. vegetable oil	1 T. instant coffee
3 lg. eggs, lightly beaten	1/4 c. sifted powdered sugar
Vegetable cooking spray	Chocolate shavings for garnish

COAT two 8-inch cake pans with cooking spray; line pans with waxed paper and coat with cooking spray.

COMBINE brownie mix and next 3 ingredients; stir in pecans. Spread batter evenly into prepared pans.

BAKE at 350° for 25 minutes. Let cool in pans on wire racks 5 minutes; invert onto wire racks. Carefully remove waxed paper and let cake layers cool completely on wire racks.

COMBINE whipping cream and coffee granules, stirring well. Beat at medium speed of an electric mixer until foamy; gradually add powdered sugar, beating until stiff peaks form. Spread whipped cream mixture between layers and on top and sides of cake.

COVER and chill 1 to 2 hours.

GARNISH, if desired.

YIELD: 1 (2-layer) cake.

Brownie Pie

1 c. sugar	1 tsp. vanilla extract
1/2 c. all-purpose flour	Pinch of salt
1/4 c. cocoa	1/2 c. chopped pecans or
1/2 c. butter or margarine,	walnuts
softened	Whipped cream or ice cream
2 eggs	

COMBINE first 7 ingredients; beat 4 minutes at medium speed of an electric mixer. Stir in pecans.

SPREAD batter evenly in a buttered 9-inch pie plate.

BAKE at 325° for 35 to 40 minutes, or until a toothpick inserted in center comes out clean.

SERVE with whipped cream or ice cream.

YIELD: 1 (9-inch) pie.

Desserts

Cheddar Pear Pie

4 lg. ripe pears, peeled &
    thinly sliced
1/3 c. sugar

1 T. cornstarch
1/8 tsp. salt
1 unbaked pastry shell (9")

TOPPING:
1/2 c. shredded Cheddar
    cheese
1/2 c. all-purpose flour

1/4 C. butter or margarine,
    melted
1/4 c. sugar
1/4 tsp. salt

IN a bowl, combine pears, sugar, cornstarch and salt. Pour into pastry shell.
COMBINE topping ingredients until crumbly; sprinkle over filling.
BAKE at 425° for 25 to 30 minutes, or until crust is golden and cheese is melted.
COOL on a wire rack for 10 minutes.
SERVE warm.
STORE in the refrigerator.
YIELD: 6 to 8 servings.

Chocolate Chip Pecan Pie

3 eggs, lightly beaten
1 c. light corn syrup
1 T. butter, melted
1/2 c. sugar

Pinch of salt
1/2 c. chocolate chips
1 c. pecan meats
1 unbaked pie shell

IN a mixing bowl, combine ingredients in the order given. Mix well, and pour into an unbaked pie shell.
BAKE at 400° for 5 minutes. Reduce heat to 300° after 5 minutes, and continue to bake for 1 hour, or until filling is thick. Cool on a wire rack.
Serve at room temperature.
YIELD: 1 pie.

Desserts

Chocolate Cream Pie with Cherry Sauce

1 1/2 c. whipping cream
3/4 c. sugar
2 T. cornstarch
2 eggs, beaten
1 unbaked pastry shell

3 (1 oz.) sq. unsweetened
   chocolate, coarsely chopped
1/8 tsp. salt
1 1/2 tsp. vanilla extract
Sifted powdered sugar (opt.)

COMBINE whipping cream and chocolate in a heavy saucepan; cook over low heat, stirring constantly, until mixture is smooth. Set aside.
COMBINE sugar, cornstarch and salt in a medium bowl, mixing well; stir in eggs, vanilla and chocolate mixture.
POUR into pastry shell.
BAKE at 400° for 35 minutes. Cool completely on a wire rack. Sprinkle with powdered sugar, if desired. Serve with Cherry Sauce.

   CHERRY SAUCE:
1/4 c. brandy

1 tsp. cornstarch
1 (16 oz.) can cherry pie filling

COMBINE brandy and cornstarch in a small saucepan, stirring until smooth. Add pie filling. Cook over medium heat, stirring constantly, until thickened.
YIELD: About 2 1/2 cups.

Chocolate Marble Bundt Cake

ONE devils food cake mix, prepared and placed in a greased and floured bundt pan.
BEAT together 1 (8 ounce) package cream cheese and 1/3 cup sugar at medium speed of an electric mixer until fluffy.
ADD 1 egg; beat well. Stir in 1 (6-ounce) cup semi-sweet chocolate morsels and 1 teaspoon vanilla. Spoon mixture into center of cake batter, leaving a border around the edge. Gently swirl with knife for marbled effect.
BAKE at 350° for 45 minutes. Let cool.

Chocolate Mayonnaise Cake

2 c. all-purpose flour | 1 c. sugar
3 T. baking cocoa | 2 tsp. baking soda
1 c. water | 1 c. mayonnaise
1 tsp. vanilla extract

IN a large mixing bowl, combine flour, sugar, cocoa and baking soda. Add water, mayonnaise and vanilla; beat at medium speed until thoroughly combined. Pour into a greased 9-inch square baking pan. BAKE at 350° for 30 to 35 minutes, or until cake tests done. Cool completely.

BROWN SUGAR FROSTING: 1/2 c. packed brown sugar
1/4 c. butter or margarine   1 3/4 c. sifted confectioners'
2 T. milk   sugar

MELT butter in a saucepan. Stir in brown sugar; cook and stir until bubbly. Remove from heat and stir in milk.
GRADUALLY add confectioners' sugar; beat by hand until frosting is of spreading consistency. Immediately frost cake.
YIELD: 9 to 12 servings.

Chocolate Sheet Cake

2 c. sifted flour | 3 1/2 T. cocoa
1 tsp. vanilla | 1/2 c. margarine
2 c. sugar | 1 c. water
1/2 c. buttermilk | 1 tsp. baking soda
1/2 tsp. salt | 2 eggs

GREASE and flour a 10x15-inch jellyroll pan.
IN a saucepan, put cocoa, margarine and water.
BRING to a boil while stirring. Cool, and add buttermilk, eggs and vanilla.
ADD this to sifted dry ingredients and beat for 2 minutes.
BAKE at 350° for 20 minutes.

FROSTING: | 1/3 c. milk
1/2 c. margarine | 3 1/2 T. cocoa

BRING this to a boil. Add powdered sugar to thicken. Add 1 teaspoon vanilla.

Desserts

Chocolate Praline Pie

2 eggs
1/2 c. sugar
2 T. praline liqueur

1 (6 oz.) pkg. semi-sweet
   chocolate pieces
1 c. chopped pecans
1 (9") unbaked pastry shell

COMBINE first 4 ingredients; beat at medium speed of an electric mixer until blended.
STIR in chocolate morsels and pecans.
POUR into pastry shell.
BAKE at 350° for 30 minutes.
SERVE with ice cream, if desired.
YIELD: 1 (9-inch) pie.

Chocolate Spoon Pie

1/2 c. butter or margarine
1 (1 oz.) sq. unsweetened
   chocolate
1 c. sugar

1/2 c. all-purpose flour
1 tsp. vanilla extract
2 lg. eggs, lightly beaten
Ice cream

MELT butter and chocolate in a saucepan over low heat, stirring often; remove from heat.
STIR in sugar and next 3 ingredients.
POUR batter into a greased 8-inch square pan.
BAKE at 325° for 22 minutes (do not overbake).
SERVE warm with ice cream.
YIELD: 9 servings.

THIS dessert is much too rich to slice as a pie, it is easiest to spoon out like a cobbler, and top with your choice of ice cream.

Cinnamon Ice Cream

1 qt. vanilla ice cream,
   slightly softened

1 tsp. ground cinnamon
Hot fudge topping

STIR together ice cream and cinnamon in a large bowl; refreeze.
SCOOP into serving dishes and drizzle with fudge topping.
YIELD: 4 servings.

Coconut Macaroons

1 1/3 c. flaked coconut	1/3 c. sugar
2 egg whites	2 T. all-purpose flour
1/2 tsp. vanilla extract	1/8 tsp. salt

COMBINE ingredients; stir well.
DROP by level tablespoonfuls onto a cookie sheet.
BAKE at 350° for 20 minutes. Cool.
YIELD: 1 dozen.

Colorado Creme

1 T. unflavored gelatin	1 1/2 c. sour cream
2 c. heavy cream	Fresh berries: strawberries,
1 tsp. pure vanilla extract	blueberries or raspberries
1/2 c. sugar	

IN medium saucepan, mix gelatin, sugar and heavy cream, stirring until sugar dissolves.
CONTINUE stirring over low heat until slightly thickened.
REMOVE from heat and fold in sour cream and extract. Pour into custard cups or pots de creme.
CHILL 2 to 3 hours. Just before serving, spoon fresh berries on top.

Fresh or Frozen Blueberry Pie

NOTE: You may use refrigerated pie crusts already packaged; takes 2 crusts.

4 c. blueberries, fresh or frozen (no need to defrost)	1 T. butter
	3/4 c. sugar
	3 1/2 T. flour
Pinch of salt	Squeeze of fresh lemon juice

IN a large bowl, mix sugar, flour and salt. Add blueberries and lemon juice; mix well.
POUR mixture into pie plate lined with premixed crust, and dot with butter. Add top crust, cut vents.
BAKE at 425° for 10 minutes, lower heat to 325° and bake 40 minutes, or until top is brown.
SERVE with vanilla ice cream.

Desserts

Hot Fudge Pudding

1 c. self-rising flour	1 3/4 c. sugar
1/4 c. cocoa, divided	1/2 c. milk
2 T. butter, melted	1 tsp. vanilla extract
Pinch of salt	1 1/2 c. hot water
Whipped cream or ice cream	
to top pudding, if desired	

COMBINE flour, 3/4 cup sugar and 2 tablespoons cocoa; stir in milk, butter and vanilla. Pour mixture into a 9-inch square baking pan.
COMBINE remaining cup of sugar, remaining 2 tablespoons cocoa, and salt; sprinkle over flour mixture. Pour water over top; bake at 350° for 30 minutes.
SERVE warm with whipped cream or ice cream, if desired.
YIELD: 6 servings.

Ice Cream with Caramel Sauce

3/4 c. butter or margarine	1 c. whipping cream
1 1/2 c. firmly-packed brown	
sugar	

COMBINE butter and brown sugar in a heavy saucepan; cook over medium heat, stirring constantly, until sugar dissolves.
GRADUALLY add whipping cream; cook, stirring constantly, until mixture comes to a boil. Remove from heat and let cool slightly.
SERVE warm.
YIELD: 2 1/2 cups.

Key Lime Pie

1 3/4 c. sweetened
    condensed milk
4 egg yolks
6 T. Key lime juice

1 (9") prepared graham
    cracker pie shell
1 1/2 c. heavy cream, whipped
1/4 tsp. vanilla
1 fresh lime, sliced

PREHEAT oven to 250°.

COMBINE milk and egg yolks in a blender or food processor on low speed.

SLOWLY add lime juice, mixing until well blended.

POUR into pie shell.

BAKE 20 minutes. Let cool, and refrigerate.

TOP with whipped cream and a slice of lime.

YIELD: 1 (9-inch) pie.

Lemon Cake

1 pkg. lemon cake mix
1 pkg. lemon gelatin
1 c. boiling water

4 eggs
3/4 c. salad oil

DISSOLVE gelatin in water and beat well.

ADD cake mix and beat; add eggs and oil; continue beating for 2 to 3 minutes.

POUR into a greased 9x13-inch pan and bake at 350° for 35 to 45 minutes, or until cake tests done.

ICING:

2 lemons, juiced

2 c. powdered sugar

COMBINE and pour over baked cake, and return to the oven until glazed.

Desserts

Lemon Sherbet

1 env. unflavored gelatin	1/2 c. skim milk
1/4 c. sugar	2 1/2 c. skim milk
1 (6 oz.) can frozen	1/2 tsp. grated lemon rind
lemonade concentrate,	
thawed & undiluted	

SPRINKLE gelatin over 1/2 cup skim milk in a medium saucepan; let stand 1 minute. Add sugar and cook over low heat until gelatin dissolves, stirring constantly. Remove from heat.

STIR in 2 1/2 cups milk and remaining ingredients (mixture will curdle). Pour into an 8-inch square pan; freeze 3 hours, or until mixture is firm, but not frozen.

POSITION knife blade in food processor bowl; chop sherbet mixture into chunks and place in processor bowl. Process until smooth.

RETURN mixture to pan; freeze 4 hours, or until frozen. Let stand 10 minutes before serving.

YIELD: 8 servings.

Macadamia Nut Brownies

2 1/2 c. sugar
1 1/2 c. unsalted butter
5 oz. bitter chocolate, finely grated

2 c. flour, sifted
6 eggs
1 c. macadamia nuts, chopped

LINE a 10x15-inch baking pan with parchment or waxed paper. Butter sides of pan and set aside.

IN a medium-size saucepan, melt sugar, butter and chocolate together, just until chocolate melts. Blend in sifted flour, eggs and nuts. Mix only until flour is moist and eggs are blended.

SPREAD batter evenly into prepared baking pan.

BAKE at 350° for approximately 30 minutes. Remove from oven and cool completely.

FUDGE TOPPING:
1 c. heavy cream

12 oz. sweet dark chocolate, finely grated

HEAT heavy cream to a boil. Reduce heat and add chocolate. Stir until chocolate melts and mixture becomes smooth. Cool thoroughly, then frost brownies.

SPRINKLE brownies with additional chopped macadamia nuts, if desired.

Orange Poached Pears

1 c. sugar
1/2 c. orange juice
6 pears

1/2 c. water
2 T. lemon juice
Twists of orange rind (opt.)

COMBINE first 4 ingredients in a Dutch oven; bring to a boil over medium heat until sugar dissolves. Boil gently 5 minutes.

PEEL pears and core from the bottom, do not cut through the stem end. Add pears to Dutch oven. Cover and reduce heat; simmer 15 minutes.

TRANSFER pears and syrup to a medium bowl; cover and chill thoroughly.

SPOON pears and syrup into dessert dishes; top each with a twist of orange rind, if desired.

YIELD: 6 servings.

Desserts

Orange Pudding

1 3/4 c. milk	1/3 c. sugar
1/4 c. quick-cooking tapioca	1/8 tsp. salt
2 eggs, separated	2 T. sugar
2 tsp. grated orange rind	1/4 c. orange juice

IN MICROWAVE:
COMBINE milk, 1/3 cup sugar, tapioca, salt and egg yolks in a 2-quart glass bowl; beat at low speed of an electric mixer until blended. MICROWAVE at High, uncovered, for 7 to 7 1/2 minutes, or until thickened, stirring at 2-minute intervals.
BEAT egg whites (at room temperature) until frothy. Gradually add 2 tablespoons sugar, beating until stiff peaks form.
FOLD in orange rind and juice. Fold egg white mixture into pudding mixture; spoon into dessert dishes. Chill until set.
YIELD: 4 servings.

Rum-Flavored Pots de Creme

8 (1 oz.) sq. semi-sweet chocolate	Slivered almonds, toasted
	2 c. half & half
1 T. sugar	6 egg yolks, slightly beaten
2 T. dark rum	Whipped cream

COMBINE chocolate, half & half, and sugar in top of double boiler; bring water to a boil. Reduce heat; cook until chocolate melts.
GRADUALLY stir about 1/4 of chocolate mixture into yolks; add to remaining chocolate mixture, stirring well. Stir in dark rum.
POUR into serving dishes, chill at least 8 hours.
GARNISH with whipped cream and almonds.
YIELD: 6 servings.

Peach Cobbler

1 (15 oz.) pkg. refrigerated pie crusts	2 T. milk
	1 tsp. all-purpose flour
4 c. frozen, sliced peaches (may use fresh)	1/2 c. sugar
	1/4 c. cornstarch
1/2 tsp. ground cinnamon	2 T. butter or margarine,
1/2 c. water	melted
1 lg. egg	1 T. sugar

ROLL 1 pie crust into a 12-inch circle. Sprinkle flour over surface. Place crust, floured-side down, in a 9 1/2-inch quiche dish. Place peaches in crust.

COMBINE 1/2 cup sugar, cinnamon and cornstarch; sprinkle over peaches and drizzle with water and butter.

UNFOLD remaining pie crust, and roll on a lightly-floured surface into a 12-inch circle; place over peaches. Fold edges under, and flute.

CUT 6 (1-inch) slits in top of pie crust with a sharp knife.

COMBINE egg and milk, stirring well; brush over top pie crust and sprinkle evenly with 1 tablespoon sugar. Place on a baking sheet.

BAKE at 350° for 1 hour, or until golden.

YIELD: 8 servings.

Peach Pie

Unbaked pie crust	2/3 c. sugar
5 to 6 sliced peaches	1/4 c. flour
1 c. whipping cream, unwhipped	1/4 tsp. salt
	1/2 tsp. cinnamon

POUR ingredients into unbaked pie shell.

BAKE at 500° for 40 to 45 minutes.

Pound Cake

1 c. butter	6 eggs
2 c. sugar	1 tsp. vanilla
2 c. flour	

BEAT all ingredients together with mixer for 15 minutes.

BAKE at 350° for 1 hour.

TOP with your favorite fresh, frozen or canned fruit; top with Cool Whip.

Zucchini Cake

3 eggs	3 tsp. cinnamon
2 c. sugar	1 tsp. baking powder
1 c. oil	3 tsp. vanilla
2 c. grated zucchini	1 c. chopped walnuts
2 c. flour, sifted	1/4 tsp. salt
2 tsp. baking soda	1 c. raisins

MIX first 5 ingredients, add remaining ingredients and mix.
BAKE at 350° in a 9x13-inch pan for 45 to 50 minutes. Cool.

CREAM CHEESE FROSTING:

1 (3 oz.) pkg. cream cheese, softened	1 tsp. vanilla
	3/4 c. margarine, softened
3 c. powdered sugar, sifted	2 T. milk

MIX all ingredients, beat well, on medium speed of electric mixer, and ice cooled cake.

Notes &
Recipes

ORDER BLANK

NAME _____

ADDRESS _____

CITY & STATE _____ ZIP _____

How many copies? _____ Amount enclosed _____
    Price per book $12.00
    Postage & handling 2.50
    Total $14.50
Please make checks payable to:
              The Machine Shed
Mail orders to: Hog Wild About Pork
              111 W. 76th Street
              Davenport, IA 52806

ORDER BLANK

NAME _____

ADDRESS _____

CITY & STATE _____ ZIP _____

How many copies? _____ Amount enclosed _____
    Price per book $12.00
    Postage & handling 2.50
    Total $14.50
Please make checks payable to:
              The Machine Shed
Mail orders to: Hog Wild About Pork
              111 W. 76th Street
              Davenport, IA 52806

ORDER BLANK

NAME _____

ADDRESS _____

CITY & STATE _____ ZIP _____

How many copies? _____ Amount enclosed _____
    Price per book $12.00
    Postage & handling 2.50
    Total $14.50
Please make checks payable to:
              The Machine Shed
Mail orders to: Hog Wild About Pork
              111 W. 76th Street
              Davenport, IA 52806